THE PICTURE HISTORY

of

GREAT INVENTORS

To the inventors herein.
And to Geraldine and Emily Carter, Alison Effeny, and Peter Turvey,
with thanks for their help.

"I see you're admiring my little box," the knight said in a
friendly tone. "It's my own invention – to keep clothes and
sandwiches in. You see I carry it upside-down, so that the
rain can't get in."
Alice's Adventures in Wonderland
Lewis Carroll

This is a Borzoi Book published by Alfred A. Knopf, Inc.

First American edition, 1994.

Text and illustrations copyright © 1993 Gillian Clements

Library of Congress Cataloging-in-Publication Data

Clements Gillian.
    The picture history of great inventors/by Gillian Clements.
    p.   cm.
    Includes index.
    SUMMARY: An illustrated introduction to sixty major inventors,
    from the unknown inventor of the wheel to today's developers of
    virtual reality.
    ISBN 0-679-84787-1 (paperback)—ISBN 0-679-84788-X (hardcover)
    1. Inventions—History—Juvenile literature.   2. Inventions—History
    —Pictorial Works—Juvenile literature.   3. Inventors—History—Juvenile
    literature.   4. Inventors—History—Pictorial works—Juvenile literature.
    [1. Inventors.   2. Inventions.]
I. Title.
T15.C58 1993
609—dc20
93-21705

Manufactured in Singapore

10 9 8 7 6 5 4 3 2 1

THE PICTURE HISTORY
of
GREAT
INVENTORS

Gillian Clements

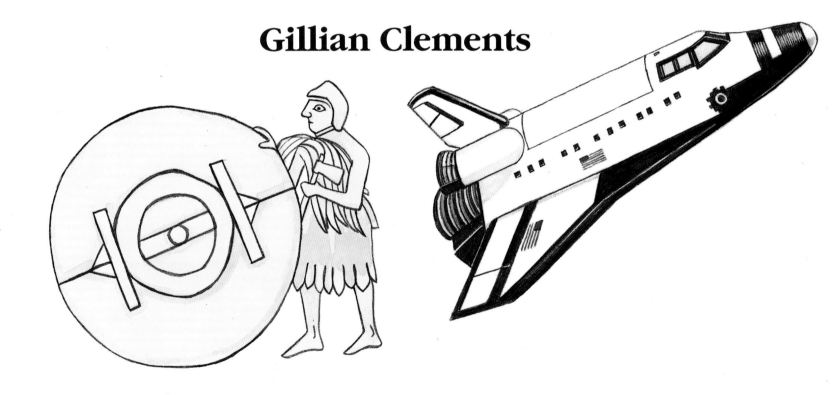

Alfred A. Knopf · New York

CONTENTS

About this book

The Picture History of Great Inventors ranges from the earliest civilizations to the present day. Although we don't know who first made a plow or who invented the wheel, we do know the names of some early inventors, such as Archimedes and Hero. Together with many of the great inventors who followed in their footsteps, they are the "heroes" of this picture history.

Most pages in this book focus on a major inventor and his work, but in the surrounding illustrations, you'll learn about other inventions that were developed at the same time. And in the timeline running along the bottom of each page, you'll get a glimpse of other events that took place during that era. For instance, when Leonardo da Vinci was busy sketching designs for helicopters and submarines, polite Europeans were enjoying a brand-new device—the pocket handkerchief.

Because historical records are incomplete, and because of limited opportunities in the past for some people, many major inventions are associated with European men. But in this book you'll meet not only the men behind humankind's incredible achievements but the women too—women like Ada Lovelace, who invented computer programming. You'll also discover little-known facts about African-American inventors such as Elijah McCoy, an ex-slave who invented a device to keep train engines from overheating. Today, women and men of all races and backgrounds must make sure that science and technology become more approachable, more welcoming, and more open to question. After all, scientists are not always right. If they were, Einstein could never have disproved any of Newton's theories!

In conclusion, a word about dates: Throughout, I've used the accepted date for an invention. Sometimes this is the date when a *patent*—the sole legal right given to an inventor by the government to make and sell an invention—was first granted. Sometimes it is when the invention was marketed and made available to the public. So, although some dates are approximate, they are as accurate as possible.

INTRODUCTION

Dear Reader:

About one hundred years ago, Henry Ford was building his first automobile and the Lumière brothers were experimenting with moving pictures. Just seventy years later—within the life span of a human being—a moon buggy rolled over the lunar landscape, and "moving pictures" broadcast images of men *on* the moon! And now NASA is planning to put a space station on Mars.

Seeing is believing. I don't think Henry Ford or the Lumières could have imagined this future, let alone believed any of these things might really happen. Yet they have happened, and the pace of change grows ever faster. Can you imagine where today's technologies and inventions will take us and how they will alter our lives? It's exciting, and a bit frightening too.

Everything around us—from the pencils we use to the satellites circling the globe—was invented by someone. And all the inventors in this book have one thing in common—they met the challenge of solving problems, of finding new or better ways of doing things. It was fun for me to learn about their struggles and achievements. I hope you share my enjoyment.

Gillian Clements

P.S. I may creep off now to some quiet corner to think about twenty-*first* century inventions. Better still, perhaps we can all become inventors and set about solving the problems of the world now!

THE EARLIEST INVENTIONS

Inventions developed as civilizations arose along the great river valleys:
in China, Mesopotamia, Egypt, Greece, and Rome.

GREECE

C.1650 B.C.	Sword
C.640 B.C.	Roof Tiles
C.500 B.C.	Catapult
C.400 B.C.	Archytas of Taventum's Pulley
C.236 B.C.	Archimedes' Screw
C.150 B.C.	Astrolabe
A.D. C.100	Ptolemy's Earth-Centered Universe

ROME

C.350 B.C.	Roads
C.200 B.C.	Arched Bridges
C.150 B.C.	Screwpress
C.100 B.C.	Concrete
C.100 B.C.	Central Heating, Baths
C.50 B.C.	Groin Vault
C.20 B.C.	Aqueduct
C.10 B.C.	Crane
C. A.D. 100	Sandglass Timer
C. A.D. 79	Drawing Compass
C.100	Pantheon Dome

EGYPT

C.5000–4000 B.C.	Copper Smelting
C.4500 B.C.	Grain Scale
C.3000 B.C.	Sailing Ship
2800–2700 B.C.	Great Pyramids at Giza and Saqqara
C.2000 B.C.	Shadow Clock
C.2000 B.C.	Bread Oven
C.1400 B.C.	Water Clock
C.1375 B.C.	Gondola
C.300–230 B.C.	Ctesibius's Inventions – Valves, Springs, Water Pump
C.285 B.C.	Pharos Lighthouse
C.100 B.C.	Parchment
C. A.D. 100	Hero's Turbine

MESOPOTAMIA

C.6000 B.C.	Bricks at Jericho
C.3500 B.C.	Kilns for Bricks
C.3500 B.C.	Plow
C.3500 B.C.	Potter's Wheel
C.3500 B.C.	Wheel
C.3000 B.C.	Arch at Ur
C.3000 B.C.	Abacus
C.1500 B.C.	Seed Drill
C. 700 B.C.	Tunnel Vault

ROME   **GREECE**   **MESOPOTAMIA**   **EGYPT**

Euphrates River   *Tigris River*

Jericho   Alexandria   Giza   Saqqara   Ur   Hero

> I, PTOLEMY, SAID THE EARTH WAS AT THE CENTER OF THE UNIVERSE.

> WHEE! WHEELS!

> I'M CTESIBIUS

> I'M IMHOTEP, A PYRAMID BUILDER

> MMM, LOVELY BREAD

> WHAT'S THE TIME?

NO ONE KNOWS THE NAMES OF THE EARLIEST INVENTORS, BUT MANY EGYPTIAN AND GREEK

Over 500,000 years ago. Fire is used for warmth.

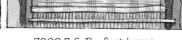

40,000 years ago. People reach Australia.

25,000 years ago. Bones are used to build shelters.

c.20,000–10,000 B.C. Cave paintings in Lascaux, France.

From c.8600 B.C. Farming develops along the great river valleys.

7000 B.C. The first looms.

c.5000 B.C. Metal smelting of copper ores in Egypt.

5000 B.C. An early form of irrigation – the shaduf.

4000–3000 B.C. Potter's wheel in Sumeria.

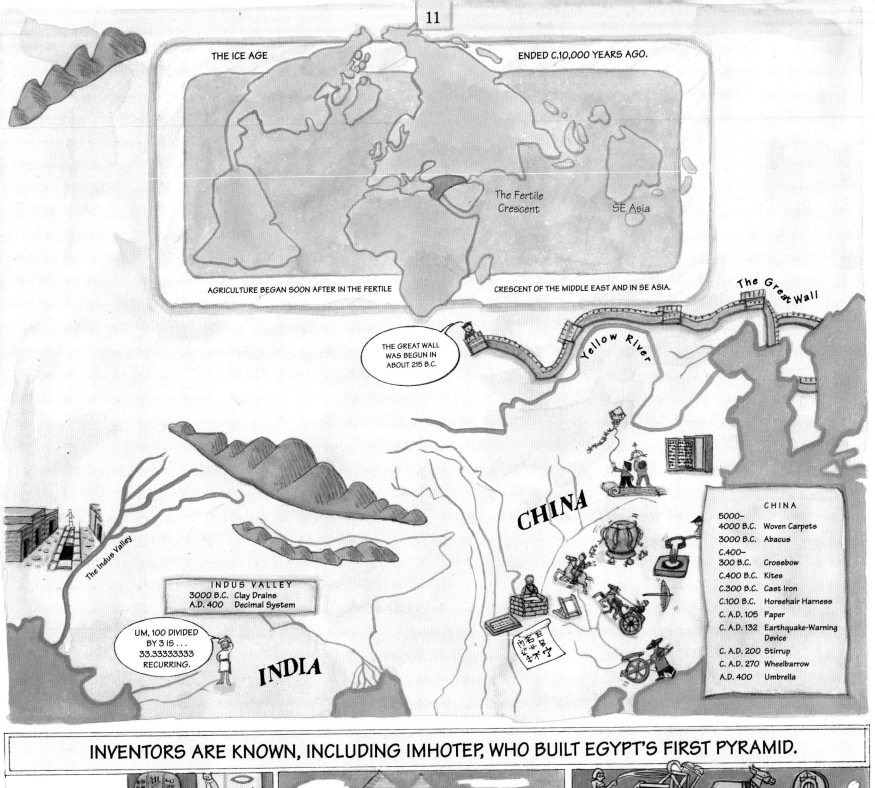

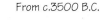
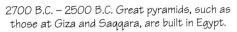

287 B.C. ARCHIMEDES 212 B.C.

The brilliant Greek scientist Archimedes was born in Syracuse, Sicily. His best-known invention was a machine for raising water, called Archimedes' screw. He is also famous for his work on buoyancy, or floating bodies, which led him to develop Archimedes' principle.

Archimedes' many mechanical inventions and war machines made him popular in his day. Archimedes' screw, for example, was used for raising water from ditches and emptying flooded ships. Archimedes also studied how levers worked and how geometry could be used to measure circles.

Archimedes' war machines held off Roman attacks for three years, but in 212 B.C. Syracuse was captured, and Archimedes was killed by a Roman soldier.

c. 100s B.C. Parchment — the dried and shaved skin of certain animals — is used to write on. Sheep skin is a main source of parchment.

c. 230 B.C. Oil lamps come into use at this time in Greece, about 18,000 years after their first use in China.

c. 100s B.C. Ctesibius of Alexandria invents the plunger pump.

c. 285 B.C. The Pharos lighthouse in Alexandria, Egypt, is completed.

Archimedes' principle: When a body is wholly or partially immersed in a fluid it appears to lose weight: i.e. it experiences buoyancy, or an upward force, equal to the weight of the fluid it displaces.

I'M BUOYED UP!

HELP!

ARCHIMEDES' SCREW

EUREKA!

CROWN

THE WEIGHT OF THE WATER DISPLACED BY THE CROWN EQUALED THE WEIGHT OF THE CROWN.

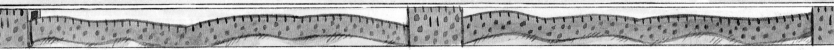

c. 215 B.C. The 1,500-mile-long Great Wall of China is built to keep out barbarian invaders.

275 B.C. The Colossus of Rhodes is completed in Greece.

c. 250 B.C. Iron Age "La Tène" people invade Britain.

c. 276–194 B.C. Eratosthenes calculates the Earth's circumference (distance around).

264 B.C. Gladiators take part in the first public contests in Rome.

HERO of ALEXANDRIA
1st century A.D.

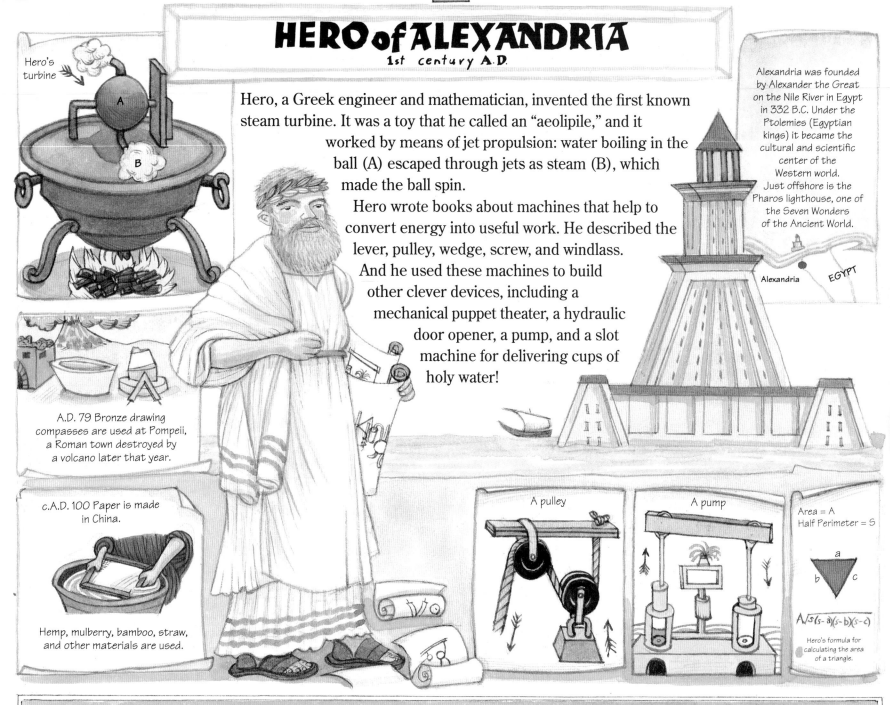

Hero's turbine

Hero, a Greek engineer and mathematician, invented the first known steam turbine. It was a toy that he called an "aeolipile," and it worked by means of jet propulsion: water boiling in the ball (A) escaped through jets as steam (B), which made the ball spin.

Hero wrote books about machines that help to convert energy into useful work. He described the lever, pulley, wedge, screw, and windlass. And he used these machines to build other clever devices, including a mechanical puppet theater, a hydraulic door opener, a pump, and a slot machine for delivering cups of holy water!

Alexandria was founded by Alexander the Great on the Nile River in Egypt in 332 B.C. Under the Ptolemies (Egyptian kings) it became the cultural and scientific center of the Western world. Just offshore is the Pharos lighthouse, one of the Seven Wonders of the Ancient World.

Alexandria   EGYPT

A.D. 79 Bronze drawing compasses are used at Pompeii, a Roman town destroyed by a volcano later that year.

c.A.D. 100 Paper is made in China.

Hemp, mulberry, bamboo, straw, and other materials are used.

A pulley

A pump

Area = A
Half Perimeter = S

$A\sqrt{s(s-a)(s-b)(s-c)}$

Hero's formula for calculating the area of a triangle.

IN HIS WORK "MECHANICA" HERO DESCRIBED LIFTING AND HAULING MACHINES SUCH AS LEVERS AND PULLEYS.

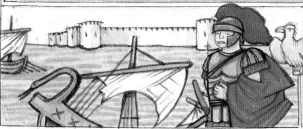

A.D. 98–117 Under the emperor Trajan, the Roman Empire reaches its greatest extent.

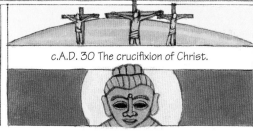

c.A.D. 30 The crucifixion of Christ.

A.D. 58 Buddhism is introduced into China from India.

EGYPT   RED SEA   INDIA

A.D. 40 Greek sailors begin a new spice trade when they use the monsoon winds to reach India.

Medieval Inventions

The Roman Empire fell in A.D. 476. A period known as the Dark Ages then began in Europe, with few inventions and few advances in learning. But the civilizations of the Arab Islamic world still flourished, and in China inventors continued to break new ground.

During the early Middle Ages, as the monasteries in Europe began to explore ancient learning, and the culture Christian Crusaders traveled to see the learned centers of Islam, a new grew and there were many inventions.

I'VE GOT THE WHEEL, BUT HOW DO I USE THE JACK?

The iron ore's burning well!

WROUGHT-IRON SMELTING

EUROPE

STAINED GLASS, AUGSBURG CATHEDRAL

VILLARD DE HONNECOURT'S SCREW JACK (FOR LIFTING OR EXERTING PRESSURE)

VERTICAL SAIL WINDMILL

MUZZLE-LOADING CANNON

EUROPE

C. 700 Wrought-iron smelting, Catalonia

C. 800 "King Alfred's" candle clock

C. 900–1000 Wheeled plows, used earlier by the Romans, become widespread

C. 1065 Stained glass, Augsburg Cathedral (now in southwest Germany)

C. 1150 Welsh longbow

C. 1180 Vertical sail windmill

C. 1200 Spinning wheel from India

C. 1250 Villard de Honnecourt's screw jack

C. 1280 Eyeglasses from Venice

C. 1300 An early clock (with verge escapement mechanism)

C. 1300 Compass

C. 1350 Muzzle-loading cannon (first invented in China)

C. 1450 Gutenberg's press

WHEELED PLOW

GUTENBERG'S PRESS

VERGE ESCAPE-MENT CLOCK

EYEGLASSES

CANDLE CLOCK

COMPASS

WELL, WHICH WAY IS IT, THEN?

SPINNING WHEEL

MANY EUROPEAN AND ARAB "INVENTIONS" HAD FIRST BEEN MADE

984 Chiao Wei Yo invents a canal lock.

c. 1000 Ibn al-Haytham invents the magnifying glass.

c. 1040–1050 Pi-Sheng uses movable type in China.

c. 725 I Hsing makes a water clock.

c. 1150–1220 Ismaeil al-Jazari makes mechanical devices.

c. 1250 Villard de Honnecourt invents a water-powered saw.

c. 1267 The monk Roger Bacon makes lenses and gunpowder.

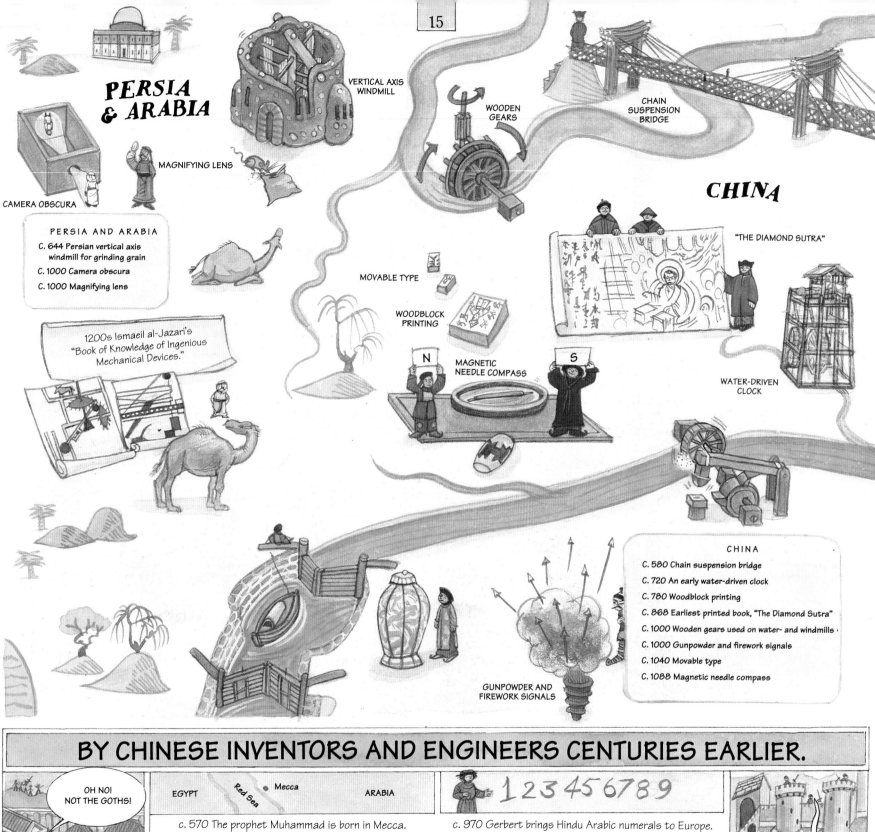

BY CHINESE INVENTORS AND ENGINEERS CENTURIES EARLIER.

c.1397 Johann Gutenberg 1468

1400s Jan and Hubert van Eyck perfect oil painting.

German goldsmith Johann Gutenberg pioneered printing with movable type, or metal letters. In the early 1450s he engraved mirror-image letters on blocks of metal, cast the letters in molds, and then cut them into shape.

To prepare for printing, Gutenberg formed words with the type and put the type into sentence or type sticks. He then clamped the sticks together and placed them in the printing press. The type could be changed into different combinations of words and sentences, inked, and printed many times over.

The development of printing in Europe was tremendously important. Thousands of books were printed, aiding the spread of ideas throughout the Western world from the 14th to the 16th centuries. Gutenberg's method of printing stayed largely unchanged until the late 20th century.

Mirror-image letter on a metal block

The letter is punched into soft metal

matrix

The matrix is placed in a mold

A metal alloy is poured in and hardens

THE FIRST PRINTED BOOK, THE GUTENBERG BIBLE, APPEARED IN 1455.

A BIT SILLY TO FIGHT ABOUT ROSES.

1455 The English Wars of the Roses begin.

1453 The Turks take Constantinople, ending the Byzantine Empire.

THE RENAISSANCE

1400s A revival in music, art, and science—known as the Renaissance—begins in Italy.

1450s Under the Medici family Florence, Italy, becomes a center of Renaissance excellence.

1431 Joan of Arc tried for witchcraft.

1452 Leonardo da Vinci 1519

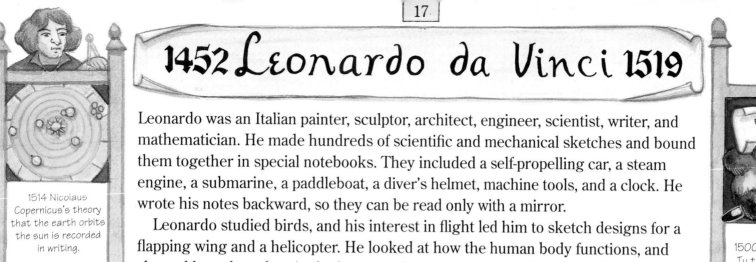

Leonardo was an Italian painter, sculptor, architect, engineer, scientist, writer, and mathematician. He made hundreds of scientific and mechanical sketches and bound them together in special notebooks. They included a self-propelling car, a steam engine, a submarine, a paddleboat, a diver's helmet, machine tools, and a clock. He wrote his notes backward, so they can be read only with a mirror.

Leonardo studied birds, and his interest in flight led him to sketch designs for a flapping wing and a helicopter. He looked at how the human body functions, and showed how the valves in the heart work almost 500 years before modern scientists did so. He invented the first armored tank and designed fortifications, war machines, and canals. Many of Leonardo's ideas were centuries ahead of their time.

1514 Nicolaus Copernicus's theory that the earth orbits the sun is recorded in writing.

1500 In China, Wan Tu tries to build a flying machine. It explodes and Wan Tu is killed.

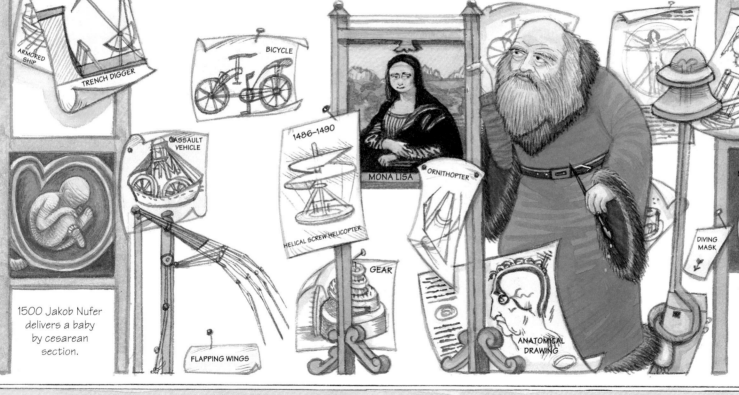

1500 Jakob Nufer delivers a baby by cesarean section.

1509 Peter Henlein makes a spring-driven clockwork watch. It is known as the "Nuremberg Egg."

LEONARDO WAS ONE OF THE WORLD'S MOST REMARKABLE INVENTORS.

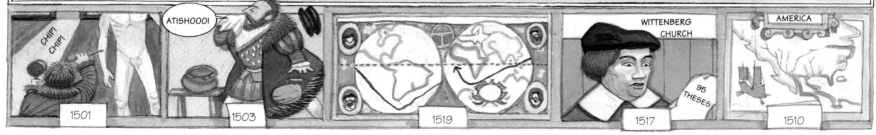

1501 — Michelangelo (Italy) begins to sculpt his statue of David.

1503 — Pocket handkerchiefs are used in polite European society.

1519 — Ferdinand Magellan sets sail on the first expedition around the world.

1517 — Martin Luther protests against the Catholic Church in Germany.

1510 — The first African slaves are brought to America.

1512 Gerardus Mercator 1594

In 1569 Gerardus Mercator, a Flemish geographer from Belgium, invented a new system of mapmaking. He created a world map that was the first to plot a curved surface as straight lines.

Mercator used advanced mathematics, but he based his work on a simple idea. Imagine a paper cylinder around a globe, touching the globe at the equator. A light bulb placed at the center of the globe casts the shadows of the longitude and latitude lines onto the inside of the cylinder. When the cylinder is rolled flat, the longitudes and latitudes come out as straight lines, at right angles to one another, forming a grid.

This new way of mapmaking meant that any constant course followed by ships over long distances could be plotted accurately as a straight line. Mercator's maps helped navigators to chart the oceans with far greater accuracy and safety.

SWITZERLAND
BASEL
LUCERNE
BERN

1566 Camillo Torello patents a seed drill. This is probably the first time in Europe that a seed drill is used for planting.

1565 Konrad Gesner of Switzerland invents the pencil. Its lead is made from pure graphite.

ATLAS

SOMETIMES I FEEL I'VE GOT THE WEIGHT OF THE WORLD ON MY SHOULDERS.

BOOM!

WORLD MAP

I AM HERE.

In 1585 and 1589 two parts of Mercator's great atlas are published. After his death his son publishes the third part. The atlas contains 107 maps.

1561 An early type of hand grenade is made for the first time in Europe; however, the Chinese began using them A.D. 1000.

MERCATOR WAS THE FIRST TO USE "ATLAS" TO MEAN A BOOK OF MAPS.

1560 Jean Nicot imports the tobacco plant into Western Europe.

Tobacco contains a poisonous substance called nicotine.

1561 Tulips reach Western Europe from the Near East.

Plan of slave ship shows how slaves were packed together.

1562 John Hawkins begins the slave trade, shipping Africans from Guinea to the West Indies.

1565 London's Royal College of Physicians allows human dissection for the first time in England.

1561 St. Basil's cathedral in Moscow is completed.

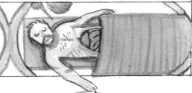

1629 CHRISTIAAN HUYGENS 1695

Dutch mathematician and astronomer Christiaan Huygens devised the first working pendulum clock in 1656. As the pendulum swung, it regulated the ticking of the clock. In 1675, Huygens designed a portable clock with a balance wheel and a spiral spring to regulate the ticking.

Huygens made his own telescope lenses, which led him to many discoveries, including the true shape of the rings around Saturn. Later Huygens studied gases, dynamics, and light. In 1661 Huygens invented the manometer to calculate the "elastic" force of gases. In 1678 he proposed that light was made up of waves, not particles, and discovered the polarization of light (the ability of light waves to vibrate in a pattern).

pump

c.1650 Otto von Guericke (Germany) invents a vacuum pump able to suck air from a globe.

1650 Hanstack of Nuremberg (now in Germany) builds an early wheelchair.

Traité de la Lumière 1690

c.1650 The "magic lantern" is made in Germany.

1658 Robert Hooke invents a balance spring for watches.

HUYGENS'S SPRING IS NOT WORTH A FARTHING.

THE HUYGENS BALANCE SPRING

BOTH HUYGENS AND ROBERT HOOKE CLAIMED TO HAVE INVENTED THE BALANCE SPRING.

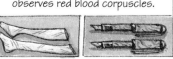

1658 Jan Swammerdam first observes red blood corpuscles.

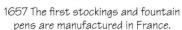

1657 The first stockings and fountain pens are manufactured in France.

GET OFF MY FOOT!

In 1650 the world's population is around 500 million.

1650 The first tea is drunk in England.

1651–1652 Dutch Boers settle the Cape of Good Hope in Africa.

1655 Rembrandt paints a portrait of his son Titus.

1564 Galileo Galilei 1642

THE COPERNICAN UNIVERSE

THE LAW OF FALLING BODIES

Venus

The Moon

Saturn

Jupiter

The Milky Way

THE LEANING TOWER OF PISA

1590

AARGH!

c. 1593 Galileo makes a thermoscope, a gas thermometer (A).

1609 Galileo's telescope (B).

A.

B.

GALILEO TIMED THE SWING OF A PENDULUM AT PISA CATHEDRAL IN ITALY . . .

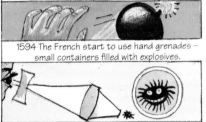

1594 The French start to use hand grenades – small containers filled with explosives.

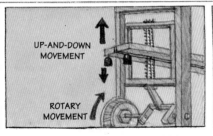

UP-AND-DOWN MOVEMENT

ROTARY MOVEMENT

1594 Davis invents a quadrant to use in navigation.

1590 Dutch lensmaker Zacharias Janssen invents the compound microscope.

1590s An ancient Chinese invention, the crank, starts to be widely used. It transfers circular movement to up-and-down movement.

1589 William Lee, an English clergyman, invents the knitting machine.

1599 A two-masted land yacht first sails.

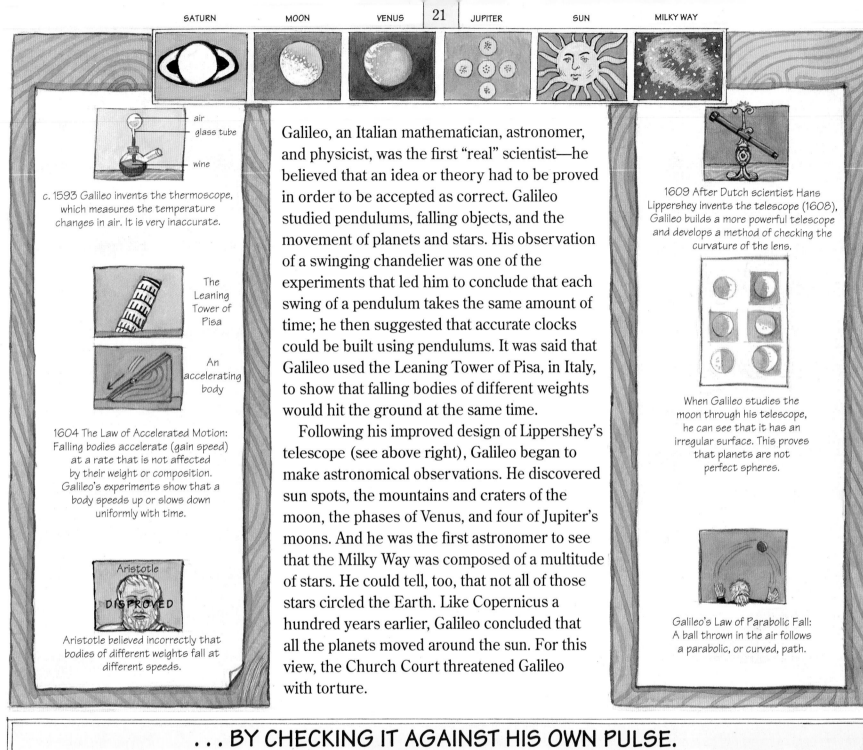

Galileo, an Italian mathematician, astronomer, and physicist, was the first "real" scientist—he believed that an idea or theory had to be proved in order to be accepted as correct. Galileo studied pendulums, falling objects, and the movement of planets and stars. His observation of a swinging chandelier was one of the experiments that led him to conclude that each swing of a pendulum takes the same amount of time; he then suggested that accurate clocks could be built using pendulums. It was said that Galileo used the Leaning Tower of Pisa, in Italy, to show that falling bodies of different weights would hit the ground at the same time.

Following his improved design of Lippershey's telescope (see above right), Galileo began to make astronomical observations. He discovered sun spots, the mountains and craters of the moon, the phases of Venus, and four of Jupiter's moons. And he was the first astronomer to see that the Milky Way was composed of a multitude of stars. He could tell, too, that not all of those stars circled the Earth. Like Copernicus a hundred years earlier, Galileo concluded that all the planets moved around the sun. For this view, the Church Court threatened Galileo with torture.

c. 1593 Galileo invents the thermoscope, which measures the temperature changes in air. It is very inaccurate.

air
glass tube
wine

The Leaning Tower of Pisa

An accelerating body

1604 The Law of Accelerated Motion: Falling bodies accelerate (gain speed) at a rate that is not affected by their weight or composition. Galileo's experiments show that a body speeds up or slows down uniformly with time.

Aristotle
DISPROVED

Aristotle believed incorrectly that bodies of different weights fall at different speeds.

1609 After Dutch scientist Hans Lippershey invents the telescope (1608), Galileo builds a more powerful telescope and develops a method of checking the curvature of the lens.

When Galileo studies the moon through his telescope, he can see that it has an irregular surface. This proves that planets are not perfect spheres.

Galileo's Law of Parabolic Fall: A ball thrown in the air follows a parabolic, or curved, path.

. . . BY CHECKING IT AGAINST HIS OWN PULSE.

1590 Shakespeare writes his first play—Henry VI, Parts I–III.

1591 Start of the annual custom of running the bulls in the streets of Pamplona, Spain.

1592 The ruins of Pompeii, Italy, are discovered by workers digging an underground tunnel.

1592 Windmills are used to drive mechanical saws in Holland.

1593 Sir Richard Hawkins recommends oranges and lemons to prevent the disease scurvy at sea.

1623 Blaise Pascal 1662

Pascal was a mathematical genius at an early age. By the time he was 19 he had made the first calculating machine, the "Pascaline." His calculating machine was operated by a system of gears and wheels. When a handle was turned, the calculator added or subtracted up to eight figures. The answers appeared in small display windows.

Pascal's work included a theory of mathematical probability that is still used today. He continued Evangelista Torricelli's work on barometric pressure and the weight of air, and was a pioneer of hydraulics and pneumatics. He also set up a public transportation system in Paris using horse-drawn buses.

A deeply religious man, Pascal was a philosopher as well as a mathematician. At the age of 31 he dedicated his life to God and wrote two famous religious books.

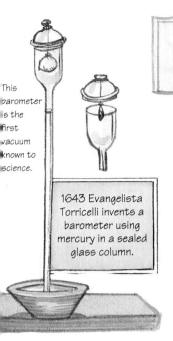

This barometer is the first vacuum known to science.

1643 Evangelista Torricelli invents a barometer using mercury in a sealed glass column.

1642 Mezzotint ("halftone") printing is developed.

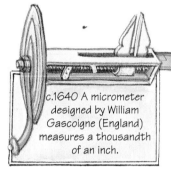

c.1640 A micrometer designed by William Gascoigne (England) measures a thousandth of an inch.

Pascal's brother-in-law helped him show that air pressure balances the height of the barometer's mercury column.

TAXES

19-YEAR-OLD PASCAL MADE THE CALCULATOR TO HELP HIS FATHER WITH TAX COLLECTION.

1643 Coffee drinking becomes popular in Paris.

1640 The first cafés in Europe open in Venice, Italy.

I THINK THEREFORE I AM

1641–1644 René Descartes writes on philosophy.

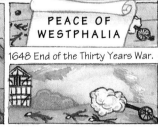

PEACE OF WESTPHALIA

1648 End of the Thirty Years War.

1618–1648 War and plague kill 9 million Germans.

1649 Pierre Gassendi says matter is made up of atoms.

1642 Tasman explores New Zealand and Tasmania.

1649 King Charles I of England is beheaded.

1642 Isaac Newton 1727

1704
Newton's "Opticks" explains that white light is made up of a "spectrum" of bright colors.

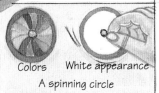

Colors   White appearance

A spinning circle

1662 Robert Hooke invents an improved microscope.

1660s Robert Boyle makes discoveries about gas pressure and volume.

1661

Thévenot invents the spirit level.

1672–1675 Gottfried Leibniz develops calculus independently of Isaac Newton.

Isaac Newton was an English mathematician, physicist, and astronomer whose theories changed the way people looked at the world. Newton spent his childhood reading and making scientific models. By the time he was 17 and a student at Cambridge University, he knew more than many of his professors.

As a young mathematics professor, Newton began to develop the rules of calculus, which helped him to work out the curved path of moving objects, such as the orbit of the moon around the Earth.

Newton devised his theories on gravity while on his mother's farm. There an apple fell on his head and set him thinking about the invisible force of attraction between objects. His theory explained why the apple fell to earth when, for instance, the moon did not fall from the sky.

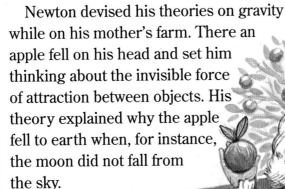

I AM OVERCOME BY THE GRAVITY OF THE SITUATION.

NEWTON'S LAWS OF MOTION

INERTIA
1. A body remains at rest or in motion at a constant speed in a straight line unless forces act upon it.

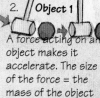

GRAVITY ACTING ON THE BODY

2. Object 1

A force acting on an object makes it accelerate. The size of the force = the mass of the object multiplied by the acceleration.

Object 2

Twice the mass = 1/2 the acceleration, if the force is the same.

3. For every action there is an equal

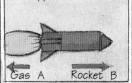

and opposite reaction.

Gas A   Rocket B

NEWTON'S DOG DIAMOND KNOCKED OVER A CANDLE AND SET FIRE TO MANY OF NEWTON'S NOTES.

1667 Robert Boyle, author of "The Sceptical Chymist," attempts to resuscitate a dog.

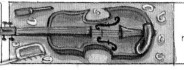
1666 Following the Great Plague, the Great Fire destroys large areas of London.

1668 Spain recognizes Portugal's independence.

1662 In France, the Palace of Versailles is begun.

1666 Stradivari makes his first violin.

1632 Anton van Leeuwenhoek 1723

Van Leeuwenhoek, a Dutch merchant and naturalist, invented the first accurate and powerful single-lens microscope—even though he had no scientific training and was entirely self-taught.

Van Leeuwenhoek was originally a draper's assistant, and one of his tasks was to examine cloth through a magnifying glass. He started to experiment with lenses and found a way of grinding them to make them more powerful. By 1676 he had invented his single-lens microscope.

Van Leeuwenhoek studied tiny forms of life and became the first person to observe single-celled animals with a microscope. He described a world of "animalcules," or "little animals"—what we today call microbes—but he did not know what they were or that they were linked with disease.

Van Leeuwenhoek's lenses made microscopic study possible. His accurate descriptions of microbes formed the basis of later medical and biological research.

WEIGHTED SAFETY VALVE

c. 1680 Denis Papin invents a pressure cooker. It is used for cooking bones.

Van Leeuwenhoek's microscope.

c. 1680 Clocks become much more accurate after William Clement and other clock makers use an improved "anchor" escapement.

1688 The first plate glass is cast by Abraham Thevart.

SCRATCH! SCRATCH!

BLOOD   BACTERIA   PROTOZOA   SPERMATOZOA   TISSUE   FLEA

IN 1683 VAN LEEUWENHOEK IDENTIFIED BACTERIA FROM HIS OWN TEETH SCRAPINGS.

1689 The Dutch hold the first modern trade fair in Leyden.

1680 The dodo becomes extinct.

1682 Peter the Great becomes czar (ruler) of Russia.

1683 The last wild boar in Britain is killed.

1682 Edmund Halley observes the comet later named for him.

1663 THOMAS NEWCOMEN 1729

Baptist preacher Thomas Newcomen, a devout Christian, made the first practical steam engine in 1712. Working as an ironmonger in England, he experimented with steam pumps to remove water from tin mines. Newcomen's invention was a genuine steam engine. It had moving parts worked by steam, and this motion in turn worked the pumps.

The Newcomen engine was a pumping engine only; the one way it could turn shafts was by pumping water over a waterwheel. But it reduced the cost of draining mines and enabled miners to dig deeper pits.

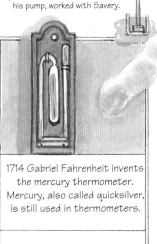

1698 Thomas Savery's pump was inefficient but protected by a patent. Newcomen, in developing his pump, worked with Savery.

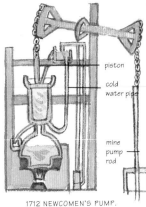

1712 NEWCOMEN'S PUMP.
The actual principle of the steam engine was first demonstrated by Denis Papin c.1690.

piston
cold water pipe
mine pump rod

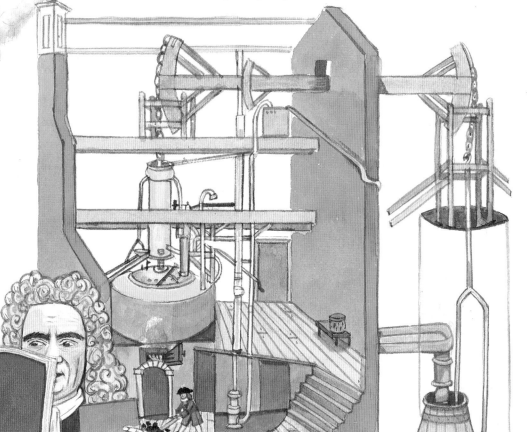

1714 Gabriel Fahrenheit invents the mercury thermometer. Mercury, also called quicksilver, is still used in thermometers.

1711 John Shore invents the tuning fork.

1714 The derrick, a mast-mounted ship's crane, is developed in France.

1721 Edmund Halley introduces a diving bell with a ventilation system.

THE NEWCOMEN ENGINE SOLD SO WELL IT WAS CALLED THE "COMMON ENGINE."

1713 The Prussian army introduces pigtails.

1712 and 1714 England and Prussia abolish witchcraft trials.

 YIPPEE  HOORAY

1710 The Meissen factory in Germany starts to make porcelain.

MEISSEN FIGURINE

1711 The clarinet is first used in orchestras.

1715 Vaudeville becomes popular in Paris.

BRAVO!

1719 Daniel Defoe publishes "Robinson Crusoe."

1706 Benjamin Franklin 1790

A LIGHTNING CONDUCTOR
KNOWN AS A FRANKLIN ROD.

Franklin's kite experiment showed that electricity produced as a flash of lightning could hit a key suspended from a kite and travel down the kite string to the ground.

Benjamin Franklin was the youngest son in a family of 17 children. He spent only two years at school but went on to become a philosopher, scientist, and America's most important statesman. Franklin helped to draw up the Declaration of Independence in 1776 and the peace treaty in 1783 following the American Revolution.

After leaving his native Boston, where he worked for his brother, a printer, Franklin moved to Philadelphia in 1723. There he founded a famous philosophical society, started a library, and established street lighting. Franklin also found time to experiment with electricity: his dangerous kite experiment proved that lightning was a discharge of electricity. His inventions included an improved heating stove and the first lightning rod.

FRANKLIN'S BIFOCAL GLASSES

IMPROVED STOVE

DIDEROT ENCYCLO

1758 Campbell invents a sextant to measure longitude and latitude.

I NEED SOME TOO!
1753 Naval surgeon James Lind (England) proves that citrus fruit prevents the disease scurvy. Sailors must now drink lime and lemon juice.

1754 The first iron-rolling mill is built in England.

1751 Swedish chemist Axel Cronstedt isolates nickel.

1759 John Harrison invents one of his four marine chronometers.

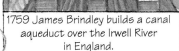
1759 James Brindley builds a canal aqueduct over the Irwell River in England.

1755 Joseph Black discovers carbon dioxide, a colorless, odorless gas.

1758 Strutt invents a ribbing machine to make stockings.

FRANKLIN WAS ONE OF THE FIRST PEOPLE TO EXPERIMENT WITH ELECTRICITY.

1750s "Capability" Brown "improves" English landscapes.

1754 The Winter Palace in St. Petersburg, Russia, is begun.

R.I.P. HANDEL
1759 Composer George Frideric Handel dies.

1759 Halley's comet returns as predicted.

1755 An earthquake in Lisbon, Portugal, kills thousands of people.

1754 The first woman medical doctor, Dorothea Erxleben, graduates in Germany.

GIVE US BACK OUR SEPTEMBER
1752 Eleven days are "lost" when England adopts the Gregorian calendar.

1754 George Washington leads his troops in the French and Indian War.

1732 Richard Arkwright 1792

In 1769 Englishman Richard Arkwright invented a spinning machine, called the water frame, that helped to bring about the Industrial Age. Arkwright's machine worked faster than other machines and could be left to spin by itself. New factories were built to house the machines, and many hand-spinners working at home were forced out of work.

Arkwright began as a barber and wig maker, but hard work and ability helped him to leave wig making behind and become a cotton-mill owner. He worked long hours and would travel at high speed between his factories in a four-horse carriage.

Arkwright was knighted in 1786.

1767 ROYAL CRESCENT, BATH
ENGLAND

1759 ROYAL BOTANIC GARDENS
KEW, ENGLAND

1762 John Roebuck invents a process to convert cast iron to malleable iron.

FIRE, FIRE!

WHO STARTED IT?

1766 Marie invents a fire escape using a basket on pulley and chains.

Arkwright's water frame was powered by a water wheel. The cotton it produced was fine but strong and good for weaving.

WATER FRAME

GOOD YARN

Spinning Machine

ARKWRIGHT
Barber   Wig maker

1766 Henry Cavendish discovers the gas hydrogen.

c.1760 The sextant is first used in navigation.

1769 Cugnot invents the steam road carriage (the first real automobile).

1764 Hargreaves invents the spinning jenny.

It spins eight threads at once.

I'LL WRITE AN OPERA TOMORROW

ARKWRIGHT WAS KNOWN AS THE FATHER OF THE FACTORY SYSTEM.

1768 James Cook makes his first voyage on the Endeavour.

c.1760 Carolus Linnaeus's important plant and animal classifications start to be used.

1762 The flightless solitaire becomes extinct.

1768 Boston citizens refuse to house British troops.

PUSH OFF!

1762 Rousseau publishes "The Social Contract."

1764 Eight-year-old Mozart writes his first symphony.

1764 House numbers are introduced in London.

1763 Pit ponies are first used in English coal mines.

1769 Napoleon Bonaparte is born in Corsica.

1736   James Watt   1819

James Watt, a Scottish engineer, invented the first efficient steam engine at a time when the new factories of the Industrial Revolution urgently needed power.

Watt began making his engines with manufacturer Matthew Boulton. Almost every new Watt-Boulton engine carried improvements. The machines used air pressure in the cylinder to make the piston work better; "sun and planet" gears turned wheels or rotated a shaft to drive factory machinery. Watt's engines enabled factories to become independent of streams and rivers, horses and windmills. Watt also invented a governor, which made sure the rotary engines worked at the constant speed necessary for driving machinery.

When Watt wanted to describe how powerful his rotary engines were, he coined the word "horsepower." A "15-horsepower" engine had the same power as 15 horses.

1784 Joseph Bramah invents the pick-proof lock.

1784 Andrew Meikle invents the threshing machine.

1788 Patrick Miller's steam paddle boat sails at 5 knots.

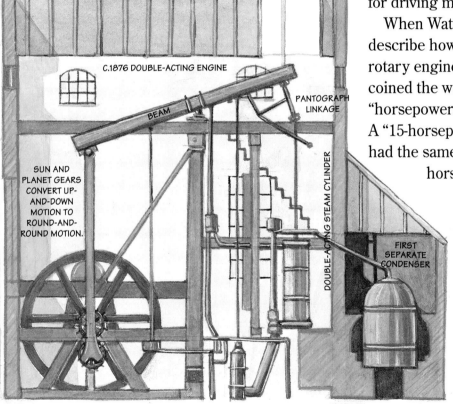

C.1876 DOUBLE-ACTING ENGINE

BEAM

PANTOGRAPH LINKAGE

SUN AND PLANET GEARS CONVERT UP-AND-DOWN MOTION TO ROUND-AND-ROUND MOTION.

DOUBLE-ACTING STEAM CYLINDER

FIRST SEPARATE CONDENSER

WATT'S WORKSHOP

1765–1769 Watt's first single-action engine.

1783 Jacques Charles flies the first hydrogen balloon.

1785 Edmund Cartwright patents the powered loom.

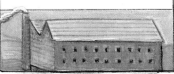

THE WATT, A UNIT OF ELECTRICAL POWER, WAS NAMED FOR JAMES WATT.

1781 Sir William Herschel discovers the planet Uranus.

1780s A growing cotton industry helps to establish England's Industrial Revolution.

1781 Britain's General Cornwallis surrenders to George Washington at Yorktown, Virginia.

1782 Boulton's Soho Works, in England, is the first factory powered by a Watt rotary engine.

1788 "The Times" newspaper is founded in London.

1789 The French Revolution begins. A mob sacks the Bastille prison.

The MONTGOLFIER Brothers

Joseph 1740-1810

Jacques Étienne 1745-1799

QUACK!

1785 Jean Baptiste Meusnier (France) develops a lighter-than-air dirigible.

1789 Frenchman Claude Louis Berthollet invents a chlorine gas bleach.

It is used for bleaching cloth.

Joseph and Jacques Étienne Montgolfier, of France, made the first passenger-carrying balloons in 1783.

In the presence of King Louis XVI, at his palace at Versailles, the brothers sent the first passengers up—a duck, a sheep, and a rooster. They rode in a cage beneath the balloon.

The first humans aloft were Jean F. Pilâtre de Rozier and the Marquis d'Arlandes. In a basket hanging below the balloon, they ascended over Paris and drifted more than 5 miles across the city in a 25-minute flight.

The Montgolfier balloon, made of linen and lined with paper, was 50 feet high. To make it fly, a fire of wool and straw was lit inside the balloon. As the air inside heated up, it became lighter than the air outside, so the balloon lifted into the sky.

We have enclosed a cloud in a bag.

1783 Sebastien Lenormand invents a "parachute" consisting of two umbrellas.

1784 Gas lamps are used to light a Paris lecture room.

THE MONTGOLFIER BROTHERS INVENTED THE HOT-AIR BALLOON.

1785 De Rozier becomes the first victim of balloon flight. The hydrogen gas catches fire over Boulogne, France.

1789 George Washington becomes the first president of the United States.

1788 Britain establishes a convict settlement in Australia.

1787 Balloonist Jacques Charles devises Charles's Law.

IF GAS IS HELD AT A CONSTANT PRESSURE, ITS VOLUME IS DIRECTLY PROPORTIONAL TO ITS ABSOLUTE TEMPERATURE.

1743 ANTOINE LAVOISIER 1794

French scientist Antoine Lavoisier is considered a founder of modern chemistry. He devised the way of defining chemical elements still used today. He also wrote a textbook called "Elements of Chemistry" and helped to introduce the metric system.

Lavoisier studied the composition of air—he showed that it was a chemical reaction involving a gas he called oxygen. As well as demonstrating the importance of oxygen for combustion, he discovered its importance in respiration.

Lavoisier worked to improve social conditions in France, but during the French Revolution, when the poor rebelled against rich people and nobles, he was executed because he had once been a royal tax collector.

1792 Claude Chappé's mechanical semaphore is used.

HA HA

1799 Sir Humphry Davy organizes "hilarious" gatherings and discovers that nitrous oxide is a painkiller.

Respiration

Heating a metal oxide

Breaking water down

The metric system

1791 Galvani experiments with "animal electricity."

1793 Eli Whitney invents the cotton gin to separate cotton from its seeds.

1792 William Murdock makes methane gas from heated coal.

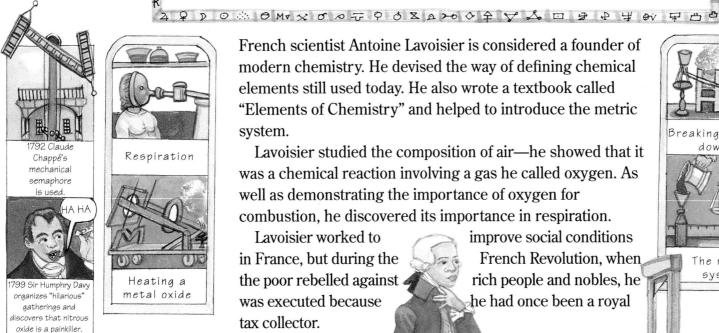

GEORGE JACQUES DANTON
MAXIMILIEN ROBESPIERRE 1794
CHARLOTTE CORDAY 1793
MADAME DU BARRY 1793
MARIE ANTOINETTE 1793
KING LOUIS XVI 1793

EXECUTIONS

ELEMENTS OF CHEMISTRY

TABLE OF 31 CHEMICAL ELEMENTS

Antoine LAVOISIER

BONJOUR

ANTOINE LAVOISIER WAS GUILLOTINED ON MAY 8, 1794.

KEEP OFF THE GRASS

1790 Joseph Guillotin, a French physician, invents a "humane" instrument of execution.

1791 Fleeing French royals are captured and returned to Paris.

1792 A Paris mob invades the Tuileries Palace.

COUP

COO!

1799 Napoleon leads a coup.

1770 Thomas Jefferson designs Monticello, his new home.

1791 Joseph Haydn writes the Surprise Symphony.

1799 A preserved mammoth is found in Siberia.

1791–1792 Thomas Paine writes "The Rights of Man."

CHARLOTTE CORDAY DUNNIT

1793 Jean Paul Marat, the French revolutionary leader, is murdered.

1749 EDWARD JENNER 1823

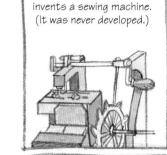

LYMPH GLANDS

In 1796 the English physician Edward Jenner gave the first vaccination to prevent smallpox, a disease many people died from at that time. Those who did survive were left with terrible scars on their skin, called pockmarks.

As a country doctor Jenner had noticed the accuracy of an old wives' tale, namely that dairy maids who caught a mild disease from cows' udders, called cowpox, never seemed to catch the more serious smallpox. To test this theory, Jenner took lymph fluid from the flesh sores of a cowpox victim, Sarah Nelmes, and inserted the fluid into scratches made on the arm of an eight-year-old boy. The boy caught cowpox and quickly recovered.

A dose of smallpox was then put on the boy's arm in the same way, but he did not come down with smallpox. The experiment was a success and Jenner became the "father" of immunology.

1795 Joseph Bramah (England) invents the hydraulic press.

1798 Aloys Senefelder invents the process of lithography.

1792 Napoleon's surgeon, Dominique Jean Larrey, designs the first ambulance to carry the wounded.

1790 Thomas Saint invents a sewing machine. (It was never developed.)

1797 Henry Maudsley (England) designs a small threading lathe that makes accurate screw threads.

"VACCA" IS LATIN FOR "COW."

MOO!

"VACCINATION" GETS ITS NAME FROM "VACCA," THE LATIN WORD FOR "COW."

MY WORK IS VERY DOWN-TO-EARTH.

1797 André Jacques Garnerin makes the first public parachute descent from a balloon.

U.S.A. WASHINGTON

1790 Washington, D.C., is founded.

1792 Architect James Hoban begins work on the White House.

VERY DENSE!

1798 Henry Cavendish accurately measures the density of the Earth.

1792 The first dollar coins are minted in the U.S.

1797 The first copper pennies are minted in England.

A VINDICATION OF THE RIGHTS OF WOMAN

1792 Mary Wollstonecraft publishes her book on the rights of women.

1745 ALESSANDRO VOLTA 1827

The Italian physicist Alessandro Volta discovered that contact between two different metals produces electricity. In 1800, using this knowledge, he invented the first electric battery—the "voltaic pile." It was the first apparatus to produce a steady electric current, and the first to generate electricity using chemicals.

Volta chose to make his battery using alternating silver coins and zinc disks, separated by wet pasteboard. He piled these 20, 30, or 60 sections high. When Volta touched both ends of the pile, he got a shock; the bigger the pile, the greater the shock. Later Volta improved the pile by using a "crown of cups." A saline (salt) solution in the cups conducted the electrical current better than wet pasteboard.

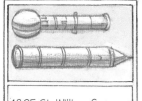

1805 Sir William Congreve develops army rockets.

THE HORIZONTAL HIGH-PRESSURE ENGINE.

BOILER

1800 Richard Trevithick builds a high-pressure steam engine.

1807 Robert Fulton's Clermont carries passengers along the Hudson River, providing the first regular steamboat service.

1801 Joseph Marie Jacquard invents a loom that weaves complex designs. It has cards with punched holes which control levers that make the designs.

MOST ELECTRIFYING, MONSIEUR VOLTA!

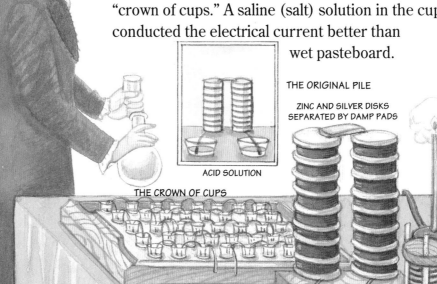

THE ORIGINAL PILE

ZINC AND SILVER DISKS SEPARATED BY DAMP PADS

ACID SOLUTION

THE CROWN OF CUPS

ZINC   SILVER   CUPS

METAL DISKS

THE FIRST ELECTRIC BATTERY

VOLTA DEMONSTRATED THE PILE TO NAPOLEON IN PARIS IN 1801.

1801 Giuseppe Piazzi discovers the first asteroid, Ceres.

1799–1815 The Napoleonic Wars rage in Europe and beyond.

1803 John Dalton (England) lists the elements, giving a sign and weight to each.

⊙	HYDROGEN	1	⊕	STRONTIAN	46
⊘	AZURE	5	Ⓑ	BARYTES	68
○	CARBON	54	Ⓘ	IRON	50
⊗	OXYGEN	7	Ⓩ	ZINC	56
⊕	PHOSPHOROUS	9	Ⓒ	COPPER	56
⊕	SULFUR	13	Ⓛ	LEAD	90
⊖	MAGNESIA	20	Ⓢ	SILVER	190
⊕	LIME	24	⊛	GOLD	190
⊕	SODA	28	Ⓟ	PLATINA	190
⊕	POTASH	42	⊛	MERCURY	167

1804 Beethoven dedicates his Third Symphony, the "Eroica," to Napoleon.

1785 Baron von Drais von Sauerbronn 1851

Karl von Drais von Sauerbronn presented the first recognizable modern bicycle in Frankfurt, Germany, and Paris in 1817. His pedal-less, wooden "draisine," also called a "dandy horse," was propelled by pushing the feet against the ground. The dandy horse became especially popular in England, where an improved version, the "hobby horse," was introduced in 1819. It had an adjustable seat and a chest pad for better pushing leverage.

The dandy horse was never intended to be a serious form of transportation—it was built mainly for amusement.

TICK, TOCK!

1814 German Johann Maelzel invents a metronome to beat musical time.

I CAN HEAR TICKING.

1816 French doctor René Laënnec invents a single-tube stethoscope for listening to the heart, lungs, and blood vessels.

1815 Sir Humphry Davy invents a safety lamp to use in coal mines.

ABOUT TIME TOO!

Canaries are used to test for methane in coal mines.

DEAD CANARY

1816 Scottish scientist David Brewster makes a kaleidoscope.

THE ART OF PRESERVING ALL KINDS OF ANIMAL & VEGETABLE SUBSTANCES

1810 Nicolas Appert (France) wins a prize for demonstrating how heat sterilization can preserve bottled food.

SAUERBRONN'S IDEA FOR TWO-WHEELED TRANSPORTATION WAS REVOLUTIONARY.

1811 Twelve-year-old Mary Anning discovers an ichthyosaur fossil.

THE GEOLOGICAL MAP OF ENGLAND

1815 William Smith (England) is the first to identify rocks by fossil types.

SAY, WHERE'S OUR SUMMER GONE?

1815 An Indonesian volcano erupts and kills thousands, and the dust fallout lowers world temperatures.

1814 British forces burn Washington, D.C.

BANG

BOOM AAGH

1815 At the Battle of Waterloo, Blücher and Wellington defeat Napoleon.

WHAT WAS THAT?

1819 Beethoven goes deaf.

1792 Charles Babbage 1871

English mathematician Charles Babbage invented the world's first digital computer, the mechanical "analytical engine." As a young man he made barrel organs for a hobby. These worked by pushing air through holes punched in cardboard, which blew each pipe at the right moment needed to play the tune. Why not, Babbage thought, use the same technique to produce a machine for making mathematical calculations instead of musical notes? In 1822 he set to work on a model calculator that worked with levers and gears. Babbage then devoted years to developing the "Analytical Engine," which was operated by steam. This mechanical programmable computer made arithmetical calculations, stored them in a memory, and made decisions based on the calculations. The computer was never completed, and another 120 years were to pass before computers became a reality.

1827 Chemist John Walker invents the sulfur friction match.

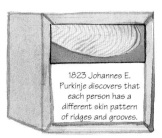

1823 Johannes E. Purkinje discovers that each person has a different skin pattern of ridges and grooves.

WHIRRR

1827 Josef Ressel invents the ship's screw propeller.

NOW LET ME SEE, WHAT'S 2 × 7?

1829 Braithwaite and Ericsson build a horse-drawn, steam-powered fire engine.

1827 Fourneyron and Burdin build a water turbine.

BABBAGE'S PROGRAMMABLE COMPUTER HAD THOUSANDS OF MOVING PARTS.

KEEP OUT OF OUR HEMISPHERE!

1823 President James Monroe issues a warning doctrine to Europeans.

1829 Hydrotherapy—the treatment of diseases with water—is developed by Vincenz Priessnitz.

free-dom fighter Simón Bolívar

1820s South American countries win freedom from Spain and Portugal.

ROAR!

BAA!

1829 Britain's Royal Zoological Society takes over the menagerie at the Tower of London.

OH DEAR, WHERE WILL IT ALL END?

1822 Franz Schubert begins his Unfinished Symphony.

1766 Charles Macintosh 1843

TECHNOLOGY

1829 Jacob Bigelow coins the word "TECHNOLOGY."

1826 Thomas Telford's single-span Menai Strait bridge in Wales is a breakthrough in modern bridge construction.

Charles Macintosh was a Scottish chemist who invented a weatherproof fabric, the basis of the raincoat that now bears his name.

In 1819 Macintosh discovered that rubber would dissolve in a coal-tar product called naphtha, and that this solution could be painted onto pieces of wool cloth. When two pieces of the treated cloth were pressed together, Macintosh found that they produced a fabric that was waterproof and could be tailored into a garment.

In 1830 Macintosh and his partner, Thomas Hancock, began to manufacture ready-to-wear raincoats.

1825 Michel Eugène Chevreul and Joseph Louis Gay-Lussac patent fatty-acid candles. They are more popular than tallow candles.

1825 John George Appolt invents the laboratory chamber gas-producing retort.

1825 Thomas Drummond invents limelight, an intense beam of focused light.

1820 Hans Oersted discovers that electric current flowing through a wire will deflect a compass needle.

MACINTOSH'S FACTORY

Macintosh's sandwich of naphtha and latex between fabric.

MACINTOSHES WERE CRITICIZED FOR BEING SMELLY AND LOOKING LIKE SACKS!

1822 Bullock explores Mexico's Aztec ruins and brings back Aztec relics to England.

TEOTIHUACAN CITY

1821 Jean François Champollion makes the first translation of Egyptian hieroglyphics using the famous Rosetta stone.

AND ABOUT TIME TOO!

1821 The Catholic church removes its ban on teaching the Copernican system.

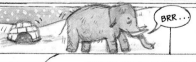

BRR...

1821 Ignatz Venetz says that most of Europe was once covered by glaciers.

THAT'S SILLY. THEY'LL BE SAYING THERE'S A HOLE IN THE OZONE LAYER NEXT!

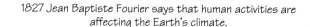

1827 Jean Baptiste Fourier says that human activities are affecting the Earth's climate.

1765 Joseph Nicéphore Niepce 1833

In 1816 Frenchman Joseph Nicéphore Niepce took a picture from his workroom window with a camera obscura—an early type of camera—and created the world's first positive photographic image. The image faded quickly.

Ten years later Niepce produced a permanent, or fixed, photographic image; it was the world's first photograph. In order to create his photograph, he placed light-sensitive paper in a camera obscura and positioned the camera in front of his attic window. The exposure took many hours, and the photograph itself was dark and blurred.

A few years after his death, his friend and partner, Louis Daguerre, discovered how to make sharp, clear photographs with an exposure time lasting only a few minutes. Daguerre made his fortune on this process.

TO MEASURE ELECTRIC CURRENT IN A CIRCUIT.

1820 Johann Schweigger (Germany) builds the first galvanometer.

PATENT No. 1
TYPEWRITER

1829 Burt is granted the first patent for a typewriter.

CAMERA OBSCURA

Acid for retouching photographs

Judean bitumen

SOLVENT

glass

NIEPCE

DAGUERRE

WHY SHOOT NEEDLES?

1829 Johann Nikolaus Von Drayse invents a gun with a needle-shaped firing pin.

A PRINTER'S MATRIX

1829 Printer Claude Genoux invents the papier-mâché matrix.

Paper treated with "Judean bitumen" is kept from the light.

LIGHT-SENSITIVE PAPER INSIDE

NIEPCE'S FIRST PHOTOGRAPH HAD AN EXPOSURE TIME OF OVER 8 HOURS.

1829 Louis Braille invents a reading system for the blind.

STOP THIEF!

1825 The Erie Canal in New York is opened.

1829 A centralized Metropolitan Police force is started in London.

Policemen are called "Bobbies" or "Peelers" after English politician Robert Peel.

1815–1822 Brighton's Royal Pavilion is built for the English Prince Regent.

GEORGE STEPHENSON

George
1781 - 1848

Robert
1803 - 1859

British engineer George Stephenson went to work in a coal mine when he was only seven years old. Almost 40 years later, in 1825, he was to see his Locomotive No.1 run on the first public railroad. Four years later, in 1829, George and his son, Robert, built the famous Rocket, which traveled 36 miles per hour—faster than any other engine.

Railroads were an important 19th-century invention. They enabled people to travel long distances with ease for the first time, and allowed raw materials and goods to be transported cheaply and quickly. Before the railroads, long journeys over land had been taken by stagecoach, which was slow, uncomfortable, and expensive.

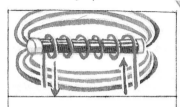

1825 William Sturgeon (England) makes the first electromagnet.

GLASS BEAD

1828 Samuel Jones patents the "promethean match," a glass bead containing acid and used, like other matches, to create a flame.

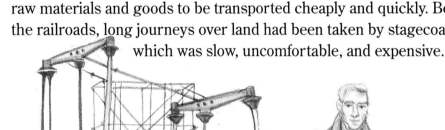

LOCOMOTIVE NO.1

1822 Augustin Fresnel perfects lenses for lighthouses.

HUSKISSON'S DYING WORDS:

"OUCH."

1830 The politician William Huskisson is killed at the opening of Stephenson's Liverpool-to-Manchester Railway.

1829 STEPHENSON'S ROCKET WAS THE FIRST REALLY SUCCESSFUL STEAM ENGINE.

1824 J.L. Prévost and J.B. Dumas prove that sperm is essential for fertilization.

1828 Karl von Baer establishes the science of embryology—the study of an organism's early stages.

L. CHAD

1823 Walter Oudney is the first European to see Africa's Lake Chad.

1829 Karl Baedeker publishes the first of his famous travel guides.

BAEDEKER'S GUIDE NO.1

BUT DOES IT TELL YOU HOW TO FIND LAKE CHAD?

1825 Tea roses from China are introduced into Europe.

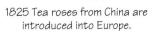

1791 SAMUEL MORSE 1872

Telegraph wires.

A B C D
E F G
H I J K
L M N
O P
S
V W

Samuel Morse was a well-known American painter. During a voyage from London to New York he became fascinated by the problems of passing messages by wire. Morse set to work to solve the problem and developed an idea for sending messages by transmitting electrical pulses along a wire. By 1837 Morse had created a working model of the "electric telegraph." Soon his telegraph lines spanned the United States.

In 1838 Morse devised a system of dots and dashes, the famous Morse code; this allowed long and short electric signals sent along wires to be translated into letters of the alphabet. His code has since been simplified but is still in use, especially in ship-to-shore radio communication.

1839 Charles Goodyear makes vulcanized rubber.

1830 Barthélemy Thimonnier (France) invents a sewing machine.

1834 Hansom cabs appear on British streets.

IT'S BURGLAR-PROOF!

1835 Charles Chubb's new safe.

1836 Beer and Mädler make the first accurate moon map.

THE MORSE KEY

For transmitting the electrical code along wires

IN 1844 MORSE SENDS HIS FIRST MESSAGE, WHICH READS "WHAT HATH GOD WROUGHT."

1844 THE FIRST AMERICAN TELEGRAPH LINE: WASHINGTON TO BALTIMORE.

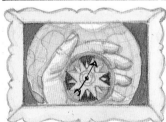

1831 Sir James Clark Ross finds the position of the North Pole.

1833 A huge meteor shower is seen over the United States.

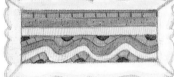

1830–1833 "The Principles of Geology," Sir Charles Lyell's study of rocks, explains how gradual changes shaped Earth.

The SS Royal William

1833 The SS Royal William makes the first Atlantic crossing using only steam power.

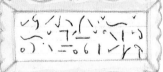

1837 Sir Isaac Pitman devises shorthand.

Another form of short hand

1811 SAMUEL COLT 1862

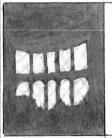

1841 William Fox Talbot patents the calotype—a negative–positive process to make photographic images.

THE CALOTYPE OF A WINDOW

The most famous Colt pistol, popular in the Wild West, was the six-shot single-action Peacemaker model.

1830 Edwin Budding invents a lawnmower.

BANG!!

1831 Cyrus McCormick invents a reaping machine.

At the age of 16, Samuel Colt ran away to sea. While there, he made his first model wooden revolver. He was still a young man when he put his hobby to practical use, developing a hand-held gun able to fire six bullets without reloading. The gun had a cartridge cylinder that turned when the hammer was cocked.

Colt patented his idea in 1835 and 1836, but success came slowly. Finally, in 1847, the U.S. Government ordered 1,000 pistols, and from then on Colt's armory business flourished. His revolvers were used during the Civil War and in the Wild West. Other work by Colt included a design for an electrically controlled naval mine, the first to use remote control.

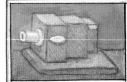

1839 Louis Daguerre devises a photographic process that makes high-quality images.

The copper photographic plate is coated with silver and iodine.

"Daguerreotypomania" spreads around the world.

1835 Ada, Countess Lovelace, daughter of the poet Lord Byron, writes the first computer program.

1839 Kirkpatrick Macmillan builds a velocipede, the first bicycle.

THE COLT, OR SIX-SHOOTER, WAS BUFFALO BILL'S FAVORITE WEAPON.

The 1830s see the beginning of a great era of railroad-building in the United States, Britain, and Europe.

1834 Both of Britain's houses of Parliament burn down.

In the 1830s white settlers travel west and move the Native Americans from their land.

1833 Slavery is abolished in the British Empire.

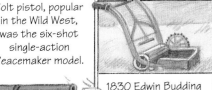

1791 Michael Faraday 1867

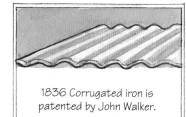

1836 Sorel invents a process for galvanizing iron.

From his humble beginnings as an English blacksmith's son, Michael Faraday became one of the greatest pioneers of electricity and magnetism. He was also a brilliant chemist and an outstanding experimental physicist.

In 1821, at the age of 30, Faraday demonstrated the principle of the electric motor. Ten years later he invented the dynamo (a mechanical means of creating electricity) and the transformer (to boost the force of the electricity). At the time, Faraday did not realize the transformer's value or its practical use, but he was able to demonstrate that if a current in a wire wound on one side of an iron ring is interrupted, it will generate current in a second wire wrapped around the opposite side of the same ring.

Faraday was also responsible for the first use of electricity to run a lighthouse. He learned how to liquefy gases, including chlorine, and in 1825 he isolated benzene.

His discoveries laid the foundation for electrical engineering.

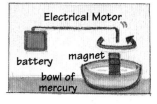

1836 Corrugated iron is patented by John Walker.

The battery produces a current along the wire. The interaction between the wire's magnetic field and that of the magnet causes the wire to move.

Joseph Henry makes a dynamo at the same time as Faraday.

1831 Henry also invents an electric bell.

fan-shaped blades

1836 John Ericsson patents a double screw propeller.

Vertical boiler installed

1836 Walter Hancock makes a steam-powered bus.

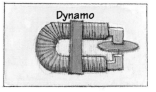

Electrical Motor

battery   magnet
bowl of mercury

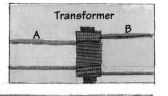

Dynamo

Transformer

A   B

THE FIRST TRANSFORMER – TWO COILS OF WIRE WOUND AROUND A RING.

WHILE WORKING AS A BOOKBINDER'S APPRENTICE, FARADAY TAUGHT HIMSELF SCIENCE.

1839 The first Grand National steeplechase is run at Aintree, England.

1830 Joseph Smith founds the Mormon church.

1838–1839 Schleiden and Schwann describe animal and plant cells.

PLEASE WELCOME JOICE HETH, 160 YEARS OLD AND GEORGE WASHINGTON'S NURSE!

1835 Showman Phineas T. Barnum begins his career.

SOCIALISM

NON! SOCIALISME

1832 The word "socialism" is first used in England and France.

1834 Henry Blair's seed drill: the first known African-American patent.

1831 Victor Hugo writes "The Hunchback of Notre Dame."

1822 ETIENNE LENOIR 1900

In about 1860 Etienne Lenoir, a Belgian-born, self-taught engineer, made the first practical internal-combustion engine. The Lenoir engine, based on a steam-engine design, used a fuel mixture of coal-gas and air in the cylinder instead of steam. The mixture was then ignited by an electric spark. Carriages at that time were normally horse-drawn, but when the engine of Lenoir's horseless carriage was started it made a terrifying noise, like a cannon firing. It was compact and convenient and was used in France and England for low-energy work like printing and pumping. Lenoir also worked on railroad signals, electric motors, telegraphy, and other inventions.

Although a system of spark ignition is still used today, at the time of his death Lenoir was a poor man.

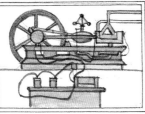

1864 Slater invents the roller drive chain. It has many uses in industry and is still used on bicycles.

Lenoir's Gas Engine

An explosion in the cylinder pushes forward a piston. A mixture of coal-gas and air is drawn into the cylinder by the movement of the piston, and the cycle begins again.

1862 Alexander Parkes makes the first plastic from plant cellulose and camphor—creating cellulose nitrate.

Long molecules

THE CELLULOSE NITRATE STRUCTURE OF LINKED MOLECULES

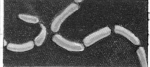

1863 Ebenezer Butterick devises the first paper dress pattern.

c.1860 Louis Pasteur demonstrates that germs cause disease.

THE LENOIR ENGINE
The first INTERNAL-COMBUSTION ENGINE that works!

THE LENOIR ENGINE, SUITABLE FOR LOW-POWER USES.

1862 LENOIR'S HORSELESS CARRIAGE WAS POWERED BY AN INTERNAL-COMBUSTION ENGINE.

1865 Maria Mitchell is the first female professor of astronomy.

1864 The first salmon is canned in the United States.

1866 A meat-packing factory opens in Chicago.

OH, MY CAMERA!

LOVELY WEATHER!

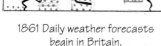

1858 Nadar (France) takes first aerial photograph from a balloon.

1861 Daily weather forecasts begin in Britain.

1865 Edward Whymper (England) climbs the Matterhorn in the Alps.

1869 The first ships sail down the Suez Canal, Egypt.

1867 The Paris fair shows Japanese art.

I.K. BRUNEL

1806   **1859**

1840 Sir Charles Barry begins building the Houses of Parliament in London.

1853 Sir George Cayley's glider first flies across a valley in England.

1845 Robert Thomson invents the rubber tire.

DANGER! NITROGLYCERINE

1846 Sobrero invents nitroglycerine.

THE GREAT WESTERN

THE GREAT BRITAIN

THE GREAT EASTERN

1843 Nelson's Column is erected in Trafalgar Square in London.

gear wheel
light beam
mirror

1849 Armand Fizeau (France) discovers a way of measuring the speed of light.

1846 Richard Hoe patents a rotary printing press.

1842 Crawford W. Long uses ether to anesthetize patients.

BRUNEL'S THREE GREAT STEAMSHIPS WERE THE LARGEST STEAMSHIPS

1843 Charles Dickens publishes "A Christmas Carol."

1845–1849 Millions die or emigrate when a potato blight causes famine in Ireland.

Ireland

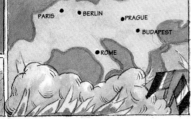

PARIS   BERLIN   PRAGUE   BUDAPEST   ROME

1848 Revolution spreads across Europe as people seek political freedom and nationhood.

1842 Richard Owen (England) first names two groups of prehistoric reptiles "dinosaurs."

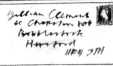

1840 Rowland Hill introduces the penny black, a postage stamp for letters in Britain.

a penny black

1835 Brunel introduces the broad-gauge railway.

1852–1854 Brunel builds Paddington Station, London.

1841 Box Tunnel near Bath, by Brunel.

1837 Daniel Gooch's locomotive, which Brunel acquired.

A man of enormous energy, Isambard Kingdom Brunel was one of England's greatest civil and mechanical engineers. He began his working life in 1825 helping his father, Sir Marc Isambard Brunel, build the first tunnel under the Thames River. He later designed and built machines, docks, bridges, railroads, stations, and even a prefabricated hospital for the Crimea (a Ukrainian peninsula).

In the 1830s Brunel designed the Clifton Suspension Bridge in Bristol. He went on to become chief engineer for the Great Western Railway and developed the first of his highly inventive transatlantic steamers. The Great Western, a wooden paddle ship, was the first steamer to provide a regular transatlantic service. The Great Britain was the first propeller-driven transatlantic liner. The Great Eastern, built in 1858 to go to Australia and back without refueling, was the first ship with both propeller and steam propulsion; it was also used to lay the first transatlantic telegraph cable.

Brunel also invented a machine to ———— dislodge a coin from a windpipe.

THE TAMAR RIVER

1853 The Royal Albert Bridge over the Tamar River is begun.

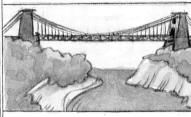

1864 Work on the Clifton Suspension Bridge is completed after Brunel's death.

1837 The Great Western is launched

1843 The Great Britain is launched.

1858 The Great Eastern is launched.

IN THE WHOLE WORLD AT THE TIME OF THEIR LAUNCH, 1837–1858.

In 1828 Brunel was hurt when the Thames Tunnel flooded.

Teams of men at work on the rock face.

The revolutionary new tunneling shield that protected workers from a sudden collapse of the tunnel walls.

The Brunels, father and son, work on the Thames Tunnel from 1825 to 1842.

1811 ELISHA OTIS 1861

1852 Henri Giffard (France) makes a large steam-powered, steerable airship.

1852 Henri Giffard (France) makes a large steam-powered, steerable airship.

1856 Englishman Henry Bessemer invents a steel-making process that allows steel to be mass-produced.

1857 Louis Pasteur (France) proves that fermentation is caused by living organisms.

HIC!

American manufacturer Elisha Otis's safety elevator made the skyscraper possible. Who would have thought to design skyscrapers if there weren't elevators safe enough to carry people up and down?

As a young man Otis built wagons and carriages, and invented labor-saving devices. In 1853 he designed a safety hoist, or elevator, with a mechanism to prevent the elevator from falling if the attached rope or chain broke. He successfully demonstrated his new invention by having an assistant cut the rope after he had ascended in the elevator.

In 1857 Otis installed the first passenger elevator, and in 1861 he patented an elevator powered by a steam engine. During those years he also designed railroad cars and brakes, a steam plow, and an oven.

GOING DOWN!

1851 New modular or prefabricated building construction: Paxton's Crystal Palace (England).

1855 The Bunsen burner, named after Wilhelm Bunsen, is invented.

1853 Frenchman Charles Gabriel Pravaz invents the hypodermic syringe.

SNIP!

KERRUNCH!

GOING DOWN!

THE OTIS ELEVATOR CO. INSTALLED THE FIRST PASSENGER ELEVATOR IN A NEW YORK STORE.

1851 Herman Melville's novel "Moby Dick" is published.

1851 The Great Exhibition in London displays the world's industry and produce.

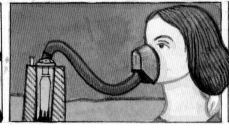

1853 England's Queen Victoria popularizes the use of chloroform as an anesthetic.

1854 Commodore Matthew Perry forces Japan to sign a trade treaty with the U.S.

1819 EDWIN DRAKE 1899

American Edwin Drake drilled the first productive oil well in the United States.

Drake started his career as a railroad conductor, but after the value of oil had been recognized in the 1830s, he bought stock in the Pennsylvania Rock Oil Company and set about learning salt-well drilling. In 1858 he started drilling for oil at Titusville, Pennsylvania, using a steam engine to drive his metal drilling tool. A year later he struck oil 69 feet down, and soon the well was yielding 25 barrels a day.

Drake's invention spread like wildfire, creating an oil boom in northwest Pennsylvania. But he had failed to patent his oil drill, and he lived in poverty for 10 years until the state awarded him a pension.

1858 An automatic telegraph system is invented by Charles Wheatstone.

1856 Mauveine is the first synthetic aniline dye to become available. In 1859 magenta dye becomes available.

1858 The first "workable" transatlantic telegraph cable is laid between Ireland and Newfoundland.

NEWFOUNDLAND

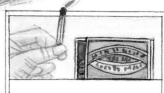

1855 Johan Edward Lundström's new safety match first gains recognition.

DOVER

CALAIS

1852 The first international underwater telegraph cable is laid between Dover in southern England and Calais in northern France.

IRELAND

DRAKE'S INVENTION HERALDED THE START OF THE OIL INDUSTRY.

ALPS

1853 The first railroad through the Alps is built.

1854 Florence Nightingale reforms nursing during the Crimean War (1853–1856).

USA

1850–1852 The United States imports sparrows to control caterpillars.

1852 Mathysen, an army surgeon, stiffens bandages with plaster.

OOPS!

1859 Charles Blondin crosses Niagara Falls on a tightrope.

1833 Alfred Nobel 1896

PHYSICS · CHEMISTRY · NOBEL · MEDICINE · PRIZES · PEACE · LITERATURE

TO MASS-PRODUCE TOOLS ACCURATELY

Alfred Nobel was a brilliant young chemist who, at the age of 16, was sent to study in Paris and America. After Nobel returned to his native Sweden, his younger brother Emil and four others were killed in an explosion in his nitroglycerine factory. Following that tragedy, Nobel devoted his energies to devising a "safer" explosive—dynamite—for use in engineering. Ten years later, in 1876, he developed the more powerful "gelignite" His inventions were used for military purposes, which Nobel disliked. With his fortune he founded the famous Nobel Prizes for physics, chemistry, literature, physiology and medicine, and peace.

1862 Joseph R. Brown invents the universal milling machine.

1868 English decorator Benjamin Waddy Maughan designs a water heater that uses a gas burner.

NITROGLYCERINE

WOOD PULP

SODIUM NITRATE

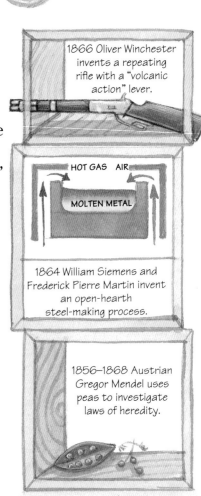

1866 Oliver Winchester invents a repeating rifle with a "volcanic action" lever.

HOT GAS   AIR

MOLTEN METAL

1864 William Siemens and Frederick Pierre Martin invent an open-hearth steel-making process.

1856–1868 Austrian Gregor Mendel uses peas to investigate laws of heredity.

NOBEL LEFT HIS FORTUNE TO ESTABLISH ANNUAL PRIZES FOR EXCELLENCE.

1861–1865 The Civil War takes place between the Union and Confederate states.

1861 A fossilized archaeopteryx is found in Germany.

It is the link between birds and reptiles.

1862 Otto von Bismarck becomes Prussia's prime minister.

1864 Jean Henri Dunant founds the International Red Cross.

1865 The Salvation Army is founded by William Booth.

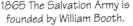

1827 Joseph Lister 1912

In 1867 Joseph Lister, an English surgeon and medical scientist, devised an antiseptic, or germ killer, for surgical operations. The introduction of general anesthetics in 1846 had meant that people could at last be operated on painlessly, but within days or weeks of the operations half of them died from infection. This infection was known as "hospital disease."

Pasteur's germ theory, developed in the 1850s, showed Lister that bacteria, breeding in the open wounds, caused the deadly infections. Lister looked for a solution that would kill the bacteria without killing the patient. He chose carbolic acid, at that time used to clean sewers and drains. His success was dramatic—both his antiseptic and his introduction of sterilized, white operating garments greatly reduced infection during surgery and saved countless lives.

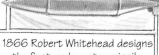

CELLULOID BILLIARD BALLS

SPECIAL PUMP FOR SPRAYING CARBOLIC ACID

EVEN IN LISTER'S TIME SURGEONS OPERATED IN OLD AND DIRTY CLOTHES.

PIPELINE

WE CAME AFTER THE NEANDERTHAL PEOPLE.

SPASIBA!

1847 THOMAS EDISON 1931

THE FIRST RECORD EVER MADE WAS OF EDISON RECITING "MARY HAD A LITTLE LAMB."

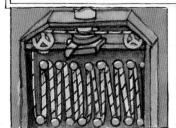

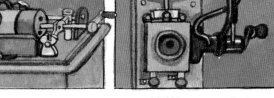

1891 The kinetoscope.

1879 The incandescent lamp.

1878 The phonograph.

1877 Improvements to the telephone.

1870 The stock market ticker.

HELLO, HELLO!
Edison's phonograph separated the parts of the machine for recording and for playing back sound. With the words above, Edison tested the machine to see if it worked, and it did! People bought phonographs for playing music and for recording conversations.

STEEL RIBS

Thomas Edison was one of the world's most successful inventors, and his inventions were to revolutionize life in the 20th century. He spent only a few months at school before starting work at the age of 12 as a newsboy on the railroad; he even printed his own newspaper on the train.

The first of Edison's inventions were a repeating telegraph, which saved time on re-sending messages, and a telegraphic printer.

In 1877 Edison made practical improvements to Bell's telephone (see the next page), and in 1878 he invented the first machine to record sound and play it back. He called it the phonograph. During that period he also introduced his most famous invention – the incandescent carbon filament light bulb.

Another of Edison's major achievements was the kinetoscope. This machine was the first film projector to produce a moving picture, and it marked an important step in the development of the motion picture industry.

Edison established the first industrial research laboratory. He called it an "invention-factory."

1873 Joseph Glidden's barbed wire makes cheap fencing available.

1876 The Plimsoll line on ships' hulls shows the safe loading level.

1875 German Nikolaus Otto's 4-stroke internal-combustion engine.

1876 Melville Reuben Bissell's carpet sweeper.

ROTATING BRUSH

EDISON RECORDS ALL OVER WORLD

EDISON'S MENLO PARK, NEW JERSEY, LABORATORY

1874 Englishman Samuel Fox's steel umbrella.

1878 Gaston Planté's 20-year-old idea for a rechargeable storage battery finally becomes practical.

1874 Christopher Sholes's typewriter. First made by Remington.

1870 Englishman James Starley's penny-farthing bicycle.

EDISON PATENTED OVER A THOUSAND INVENTIONS DURING HIS LONG CAREER.

1874 Levi Strauss & Co. begins to make riveted jeans.

1879 The Tay Bridge disaster takes place in Scotland.

1871 Rome becomes the capital of recently united Italy.

1871 Charles Darwin writes "The Descent of Man."

1875 Roller skating becomes popular.

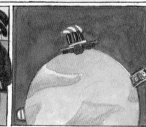
1871 Jules Verne writes "Around the World in 80 Days."

1847 Alexander Graham Bell 1922

Alexander Graham Bell, who came from a family of speech therapists, left his native Scotland and opened a school near Boston to teach speech to deaf people. One day Bell's assistant was testing microphones and receivers when he accidentally plucked at a wire. Bell, working in the next room, heard the noise clearly and wondered if speech could travel down the wire in the same way. And so he started to experiment.

In 1875 Bell tried to develop a "multiple" telegraph, which would make it possible to send several messages over the same telegraph wire. In 1876 he invented the telephone.

Bell continued with experiments to record sound and transmit sound on a beam of light. He also invented a hydrofoil boat and a kite large enough to carry people. Bell invested the money he made from his inventions in research into deafness.

1868 George Pullman designs dining cars for trains.

IT WORKS!

1869 George Westinghouse's air brake is first used.

1878 Gustave de Laval (Sweden) invents the cream separator, or centrifuge.

1877 Ball bearings begin to be used in bicycles.

1874 Solomon uses pressure cooking for canning foods.

1879 James Ritty invents the cash register. RING! RING!

Inventor Lewis Latimer, the son of an escaped slave, executed the patent drawings for many of Bell's telephones.

WATSON! COME HERE, I WANT YOU!

The urgent first words transmitted when Bell accidentally spills battery acid on his pants.

BELL USED HIS KNOWLEDGE OF HOW THE EAR WORKS TO CARRY OUT HIS EXPERIMENTS.

1871 "Dr Livingstone, I presume." Henry Morton Stanley meets David Livingstone in Africa.

1871 The Great Chicago Fire.

Jane Wells notes that babies do not sit still in seats.

1872 Jane Wells patents her Baby Jumper.

1872 The first international soccer game, England v Scotland.

1875 Giles crosses Australia.

THE REAL McCOY!

1870s Elijah McCoy's lubrication devices prevent trains from overheating.

1877 Giovanni Schiaparelli discovers a network of "canals" on Mars.

KARL BENZ &
GOTTLIEB DAIMLER

In 1885 German engineer Karl Benz invented the first practical automobile. His three-wheeled "Motorwagen" was the first successful gasoline-powered car. In the same year, mechanical engineer Gottlieb Daimler, also a German, patented an internal-combustion engine that ran on gasoline, but he fitted his engine to a wooden bicycle. A year later Daimler built his first car, a "horseless carriage" with a high-speed engine attached to an old-fashioned coach. It proved to be more popular than Benz's car, which was costly and slow.

Bertha Benz, Karl's wife, made the first long-distance automobile trip. In 1888 she set off with her two teenage sons to visit relatives 110 miles away, having left a note for her husband telling him of their plans. After an adventurous and somewhat dangerous journey in the Motorwagen, Bertha Benz and her sons arrived safely at their destination.

Monotype

1887 Tolbert Lanston patents the monotype typesetting machine. Each letter is cast separately.

1884 Lockrum Blue's corn sheller, the first of the new devices patented by African–Americans following the Civil War.

1882 Children's book writer Adeline D.T. Whitney patents her alphabet blocks with raised letters.

1889 Anna Breadin patents her "noiseless" school desk.

WOODEN BICYCLE

DAIMLER'S 1886 HORSELESS CARRIAGE

BENZ'S 1885 MOTORWAGEN

THE BENZ AND DAIMLER CAR MANUFACTURING COMPANIES MERGED IN 1926.

GIVE ME YOUR TIRED, YOUR POOR, YOUR HUDDLED MASSES . . .

1886 The Statue of Liberty is dedicated.

1885 Galton discovers fingerprints.

1887 Sherlock Holmes first appears in a Conan Doyle story.

ALL MINE!

NO, NO, IT'S MINE NOW!

I WANT A BIG SHARE!

I LIVE HERE!

1884–1885 The scramble for Africa begins.

ESPERANTO

1887 The universal language Esperanto is invented.

I'M THIRSTY!

1886 Dr. John Pemberton invents the pick-me-up Coca-Cola.

EEK!

1887–1889 The Eiffel Tower is designed and built for the Paris Exhibition.

AUGUSTE
1862–1954

The Lumière Brothers

LOUIS
1864–1948

Auguste and Louis Lumière of France developed a motion picture camera called the Cinématographe (which means "movement writer") and used it in 1895 to make and show the first film to a public audience.

Auguste and Louis were the sons of a painter turned photographer. Their Cinématographe was an important improvement on Edison's kinetoscope. The Lumières, with their trained cameramen, made 40 films in 1896 – newsreels, documentaries, short comedies, and pieces on day-to-day life in France. They traveled around the world showing their popular films.

1892 Engineer Rudolf Diesel patents the internal-combustion engine.

c.1890 Jesse W. Reno invents the escalator.

OOPS!

The Lumière Cinématographe

1895 Wilhelm Roentgen invents X-ray apparatus.

1890s James Dewar invents the vacuum flask.

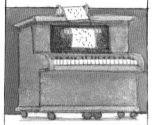

1897 Votey develops the pianola, which plays using perforated paper.

1898 Photographs are now taken using artificial light.

THE FIRST LUMIÈRE FILM, SHOWING A TRAIN ENTERING A STATION, TERRIFIED THE VIEWERS.

DEPTFORD

1890 England's first large-scale electrical power station is opened.

1892 Pineapples are preserved in cans for the first time.

QUICK, NURSE, SCALPEL.

1890 Rubber gloves are first used in surgery.

1899 The first bottles of aspirin are sold in stores.

1894 Rudyard Kipling publishes "The Jungle Book."

The Wright Brothers

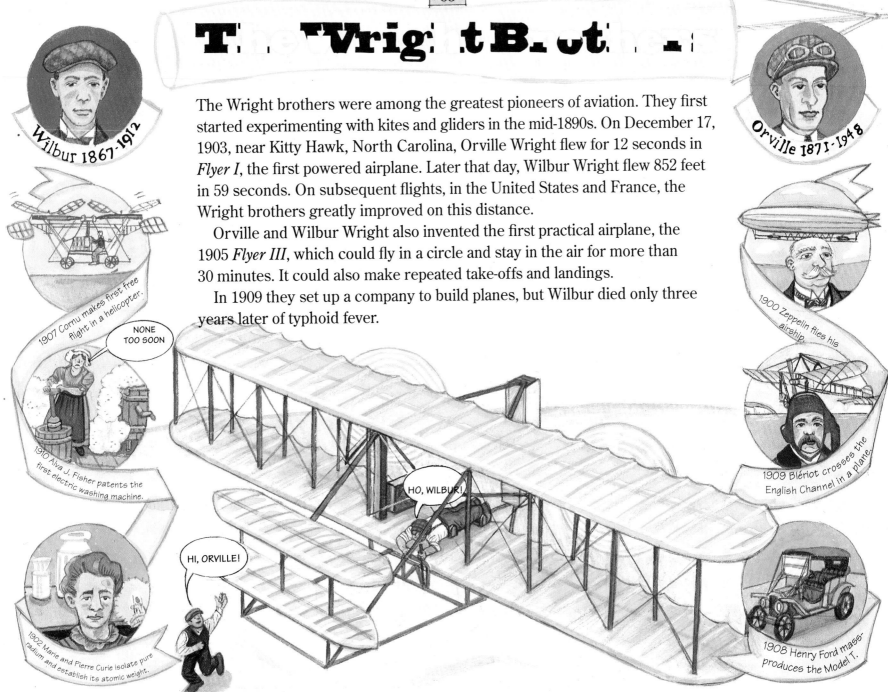

Wilbur 1867-1912

Orville 1871-1948

The Wright brothers were among the greatest pioneers of aviation. They first started experimenting with kites and gliders in the mid-1890s. On December 17, 1903, near Kitty Hawk, North Carolina, Orville Wright flew for 12 seconds in *Flyer I*, the first powered airplane. Later that day, Wilbur Wright flew 852 feet in 59 seconds. On subsequent flights, in the United States and France, the Wright brothers greatly improved on this distance.

Orville and Wilbur Wright also invented the first practical airplane, the 1905 *Flyer III*, which could fly in a circle and stay in the air for more than 30 minutes. It could also make repeated take-offs and landings.

In 1909 they set up a company to build planes, but Wilbur died only three years later of typhoid fever.

1907 Cornu makes first free flight in a helicopter.

NONE TOO SOON

1910 Alva J. Fisher patents the first electric washing machine.

1902 Marie and Pierre Curie isolate pure radium and establish its atomic weight.

HI, ORVILLE!

HO, WILBUR!

1900 Zeppelin flies his airship.

1909 Blériot crosses the English Channel in a plane.

1908 Henry Ford mass-produces the Model T.

IN 1903 ORVILLE WRIGHT BECAME THE FIRST MAN TO FLY ABOARD A POWERED MACHINE.

WE ARE NOT ALIVE

1901 Queen Victoria dies.

1907 The Cubist paintings of Picasso and Braque.

ROAR!

1903–1904 Teddy bears appear in the U.S. and Germany.

MONTANA

1908 A fossilized Tyrannosaurus rex is found.

VOTES FOR WOMEN

1900s Early Suffragists demand women's right to vote.

1874 Guglielmo Marconi 1937

Guglielmo Marconi, the Italian physicist and electrical engineer, invented wireless telegraphy and the radio.

As a young man Marconi was excited to learn of the speed at which electromagnetic waves travel through space – 186,000 miles per second – and wondered whether these waves could be used to send messages. He set to work at his attic table and made his great breakthrough by the age of 21, sending the first message transmitted by radio waves. The message traveled just 1.5 miles and Marconi's brother fired a gun to let him know that it had been received.

In 1901 Marconi sent the first radio signals across the Atlantic, between England and Newfoundland.

1904 John Fleming uses a diode (the earliest and simplest type of electronic valve) to detect radio waves.

1907 Lee De Forest introduces the triode valve. It is used mainly as an amplifier or oscillator.

1903 Valdemar Poulsen makes a magnetic recorder 5 years after inventing the magnetic recording of speech.

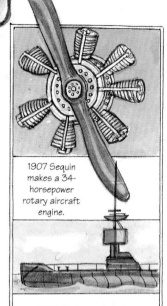

1907 Sequin makes a 34-horsepower rotary aircraft engine.

1905 Unterseeboots (undersea boats), known as U-Boats, are developed by the German navy. These submarines are used in World Wars I and II.

1907 William Hoover buys J. Murray Spangler's patent for a vacuum cleaner.

SURPRISE FOR CRIPPEN
ARREST EXPECTED

FOR THE FIRST TRANSATLANTIC RADIO SIGNAL, MARCONI TAPPED OUT "S" IN MORSE.

1910 The murderer Hawley Harvey Crippen is the first criminal arrested with the help of radio.

1904 Steerage rate tickets cost only $10 for British emigrants to the United States.

1902 A volcanic eruption and fire destroy St. Pierre, Martinique.

BEEP! BEEP!

1903 The top speed limit in Britain is only 20 mph.

1900 Freud publishes "The Interpretation of Dreams."

1857 Konstantin Tsiolkovsky 1935

Konstantin Tsiolkovsky's fascination with flight and the exploration of space began after he caught scarlet fever as a child. The illness left him deaf, and to overcome loneliness the nine-year-old boy taught himself mathematics and physics.

Tsiolkovsky became a teacher, but he remained fascinated by space and flight. He designed birdlike gliders and metal balloon dirigibles and wrote a book called "Dreams of Earth and Sky."

He understood that the rocket was the only means of propulsion that would work in the vacuum of space, and his 1903 book, "The Exploration of Cosmic Space by Means of Reaction Devices," predicted that liquid-fuel rockets could reach "outer space."

In 1957, 100 years after Tsiolkovsky's birth, the Soviet Union was ready at last to send up its first satellite – Sputnik I.

The
EXPLORATION
of
COSMIC SPACE
by
MEANS of
REACTION DEVICES

1902 Robert Bosch (Germany) invents the high-tension magneto, which generates electricity for the spark of the spark plug.

Original fan-shaped windshield wiper

1903 Mary Anderson invents the first patented windshield wiper.

IT WON'T STAIN OR RUST!

1904 Leon Guillet invents stainless steel.

1900 Florence Parpart invents a street cleaner.

1901 H. C. Booth (England) invents the first vacuum cleaner.

1909 Leo Baekeland invents Bakelite. It is the dawn of the **Plastic Age.**

KONSTANTIN TSIOLKOVSKY HAS BEEN CALLED THE FATHER OF SPACE.

1902–1903 Ernest Rutherford and Frederick Soddy say that atomic nuclei split to form other elements, emitting radioactivity.

1903 Walter Sutton puts forward the chromosome theory of heredity.

1902 Heaviside and Kennelly predict that the ionosphere exists, and Teisserenc de Bort discovers the troposphere and stratosphere.

LAYERS OF ATMOSPHERE

1901 The okapi is discovered in Africa.

AAAGH A RED TREE!

1905–1908 The Fauves ("Wild Beasts") shake up the art world.

1908 Fountain pens start to become popular.

1906 Frederick Hopkins discovers essential nutritional foods, later named "vitamins."

1905 The first neon light signs are seen.

1879 Albert Einstein 1955

. . . E = mc² mass can be converted into energy . . . all motion is relative, the speed of light is constant . . . light has mass and can be bent by gravity . . .

e = energy
m = mass
c = speed of light

light

special theory of relativity

bending light

gravity

general theory of relativity

$E = mc^2$

Max Planck

IT DETECTS RADIATION.

BEEP BEEP BEEP

1913 Early version of Geiger counter, by Hans Wilhelm Geiger.

PROTON

1914 Ernest Rutherford discovers the proton . . .

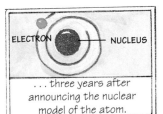

ELECTRON — NUCLEUS

. . . three years after announcing the nuclear model of the atom.

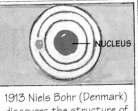

NUCLEUS

1913 Niels Bohr (Denmark) discovers the structure of the atom.

1914 Ernest Swinton develops the tank.

1913 Irving Langmuir invents the tungsten filament light.

1913 Mary Crosby makes the first brassiere out of two silk handkerchiefs joined with ribbon.

1917 Clarence Birdseye experiments with food freezing.

EINSTEIN'S THEORIES OF RELATIVITY CHANGED THE WAY PHYSICISTS THOUGHT

1914 Austria's Archduke Ferdinand and his wife are assassinated in Sarajevo, igniting World War I (1914–1918).

Much of the war is fought in trenches. Millions of soldiers die.

1912 Robert Scott and four companions die in the Antarctic after reaching the South Pole.

1912 The Titanic sinks on its maiden voyage. More than 1,500 people drown.

1913 The first crossword puzzle appears in a New York newspaper.

1917 Lenin leads the Bolsheviks in the Russian Revolution.

HELP!

1911 Leonardo's "Mona Lisa" is stolen from the Louvre Museum, Paris.

1921

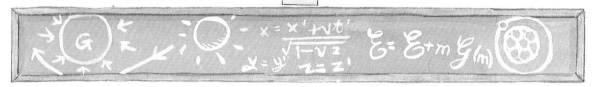

There are four known fundamental forces, or "interactions."

ALL UNIFORM MOTION IS RELATIVE, AND THE SPEED OF LIGHT IS ALWAYS CONSTANT.

The Special Theory of Relativity
1905

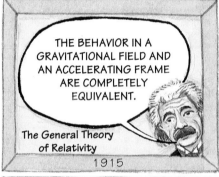
THE BEHAVIOR IN A GRAVITATIONAL FIELD AND AN ACCELERATING FRAME ARE COMPLETELY EQUIVALENT.

The General Theory of Relativity
1915

QUANTUM THEORY SHOWS THAT LIGHT CAN MAKE ELECTRICAL ENERGY FROM SOME ELEMENTS.

Planck's Quantum Theory
1905

Einstein was the most brilliant mathematician and creative scientific mind of the 20th century. His ideas about the nature of light, space, and time led to the theories of relativity and changed some of Newton's concepts of the universe, particularly ideas about gravity.

Born in Germany, Einstein became a Swiss citizen in 1910 and an American citizen in 1940. In 1905 he used Planck's Quantum Theory to explain how light could generate electrical energy when it strikes certain elements. In the same year he created a scientific sensation with his Special Theory of Relativity, which showed that nothing can move faster than the speed of light. Ten years later, in 1915, Einstein's General Theory of Relativity demonstrated that light passing a heavenly body is bent by the body's gravitational pull. And it was Einstein who discovered how nuclear power works — how an atom of an element losing mass can convert this mass into a huge amount of energy.

Einstein made the greatest scientific advances since Newton, 200 years before, and his theories inspired one of the major inventions of the 20th century, nuclear power.

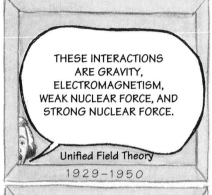
THESE INTERACTIONS ARE GRAVITY, ELECTROMAGNETISM, WEAK NUCLEAR FORCE, AND STRONG NUCLEAR FORCE.

Unified Field Theory
1929–1950

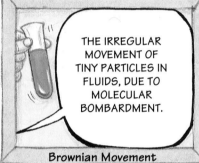
THE IRREGULAR MOVEMENT OF TINY PARTICLES IN FLUIDS, DUE TO MOLECULAR BOMBARDMENT.

Brownian Movement

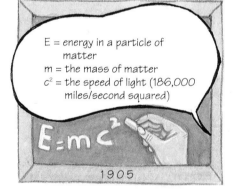
E = energy in a particle of matter
m = the mass of matter
c^2 = the speed of light (186,000 miles/second squared)

$E = mc^2$
1905

BECAUSE THEY CONTRADICTED SOME OF NEWTON'S LAWS, MADE CENTURIES BEFORE.

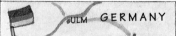 ULM GERMANY — Einstein disliked school but read as much as he could. — ZURICH BERN  U.S.A.

Einstein was born in Germany, moved to Switzerland in the 1890s, and finally settled in the U.S. when Hitler came to power in Germany.

1913 Gandhi is arrested in South Africa for passive resistance to immigration law. He returns to India in 1915.

1910 Halley's comet makes its closest approach to the Earth.

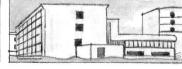
1919 Walter Gropius's Bauhaus School makes changes in architectural and arts teaching.

1917 Protesting suffragists are arrested for picketing the White House.

ME TARZAN
1914 Edgar Rice Burroughs publishes the first Tarzan story.

1888 JOHN LOGIE BAIRD 1946

Inspired by the work of Guglielmo Marconi, Scottish engineer John Logie Baird decided to experiment with sending pictures, as well as sounds, by radio waves. In 1925 he set up his apparatus in an attic workshop—using a tea chest, the lenses from a number of bicycle lamps, darning needles, wood, string, and other bits and pieces. With this amazing contraption he managed to transmit the fuzzy image of a cross to a receiver in the same room. A year later Baird was able to televise moving objects.

In 1927 Baird sent televised pictures down a telephone cable between Glasgow, Scotland, and London, England. A year later he was the first person to transmit a picture across the Atlantic Ocean.

1920 Howard invents the first Rotavator, a steam-powered rotary hoe.

1926 Le Tourneau invents the first bulldozer.

HEIGHT REACHED 184 FT

SPEED 60 MPH

1926 Robert Goddard uses liquid rocket fuel (gasoline and liquid oxygen) to launch his first rocket.

ICONOSCOPE CAMERA TUBE

1925 Zworykin produces an iconoscope in order to make an electronic transmitter, or television camera.

1920s Aerosols, cellulose tape, aerial crop spraying, hair dryers are invented.

Logie Baird's disk televisor of the 1930s, the first mass market transmitter.

BAIRD'S 1925/6 EXPERIMENTAL TELEVISION TRANSMITTER

A disk televisor picture using a Nipkow disk invented in 1884.

1925 JOHN LOGIE BAIRD WAS THE FIRST MAN TO TRANSMIT A TELEVISION PICTURE BY RADIO WAVES.

1921 Czech playwright Karel Čapek coins the word ROBOT.

1920s Modernist architecture and the new International Style.

I'M RUINED!

1929 The Wall Street stock market crash.

A "COSMIC EGG" OF CONCENTRATED MATTER AND ENERGY EXPLODES.

1927 The first BIG BANG theory. Belgian Georges Henri Lemaître says that the universe began with an explosion.

1924 Lenin, who led the Russian Revolution, dies.

MY MA-A-AMMY

1927 "The Jazz Singer," made in the U.S., is the first "talking" film.

1920 Prohibition starts after the U.S. government passes a law banning alcohol.

1900 Laszlo Biro 1985

In Europe the ballpoint pen is called a biro, after Laszlo Biro, who invented it in 1938. While working as a journalist in Budapest, Hungary, Biro saw magazine printers using a quick-drying ink. This gave the former painter and sculptor the idea of trying to produce a quick-drying pen. Soon afterward he was forced to flee Hungary ahead of a threatened Nazi invasion. In exile in Argentina, he and his brother, Georg, continued to develop his pen.

Biro's ballpoint was soon being used by the British Royal Air Force for navigational calculations. The pen did not leak like a fountain pen, even with the changes in air pressure and altitude during flight. It became a huge success, and millions of "biros" are sold around the world each year.

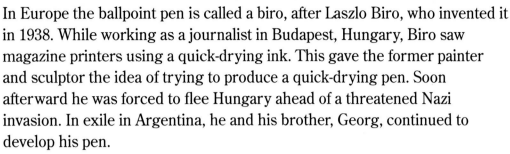

YOU HAVEN'T SEEN MY PEN, HAVE YOU?

1931 The Empire State Building is finished in New York City.

1930s The tape recorder, using magnetized plastic tape, is developed by AEG.

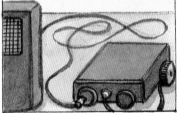
1935 A. Edwin Stevens invents the first electronic hearing aid. It has an amplifier with valves like a radio receiver.

1935 Carlton Magee invents the parking meter for Oklahoma City.

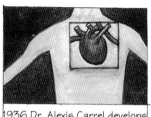
1936 Dr. Alexis Carrel develops an artificial heart.

1934 Percy Shaw invents "cat's eyes"—glass studs that reflect car headlights in the road.

BIRO'S PEN WAS POPULAR WITH BRITISH AND AMERICAN TROOPS IN WORLD WAR II.

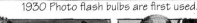

1934 C.W. Beebe and Otis Barton descend 3,028 feet in their bathysphere.

1930 Photo flash bulbs are first used.

SO EASY FOR TOASTING!

1930 Sliced bread is introduced.

1937 The Hindenburg airship disaster in New Jersey ends the Airship Age.

1933 The film "King Kong" is released.

1936 Adolf Hitler and Benito Mussolini declare a Berlin-Rome Axis (alliance).

1935–1938 Joseph Stalin stages "show trials" against so-called traitors in Russia.

1907

FRANK WHITTLE

1931 Ruska and Knoll develop an electron microscope. The microscope is improved by Zworykin in 1939.

1938 Chester Carlson invents the process of photocopying (xerography).

PATENT NO... F. WHITTLE

JET ENGINE...

English pilot and engineer Frank Whittle built the first jet engine. The jet engine was also independently built in Germany by Hans von Ohain.

Whittle was only 23 years old when, in 1930, he registered his patent. At first, the British government was not interested and so, in 1934, Whittle set up his own company, known as Power Jets, to develop his engine.

By 1937 Frank Whittle's engine was ready to be tested, and this time the British government gave him their support. For by now there were fears of approaching war, and of the rival German engine, the S3B. A German aircraft with an S3B engine installed actually flew first, in August 1939, just before the outbreak of World War II.

In May 1941 the Gloster E 28/39 flew at last, with Whittle's turbo jet engine.

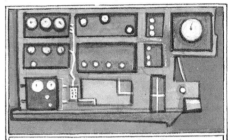

1935 Robert Watson-Watt develops a method of detecting the position of a distant moving object: radio detection and ranging (RADAR). Soon radar is used for early warning of enemy aircraft.

MAIN ROTOR   TAIL ROTOR

1939 Igor Sikorsky builds the first motor-powered helicopter.

NYLONS 1939   NYLON FIBERS   CAROTHERS

1937 Wallace Carothers patents nylon, the first successful synthetic fiber.

WHAT'S THAT DREADFUL RACKET?

MODERN JET ENGINES ARE MODELED AFTER WHITTLE'S JET ENGINE.

1933 Hitler becomes chancellor (leader) of Germany.

1932 Cockcroft and Walton split the atom.

1930 Amy Johnson (England) flies solo from London to Australia.

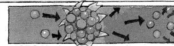

1939 Nuclear fission is discovered by Otto Hahn (Germany).

FIRST USED ON AN AMERICAN INDIAN SITE.

1930 Andrew Ellicott Douglass discovers dendrochronology – a dating method using tree rings.

1930 Pluto is discovered by C.W. Tombaugh.

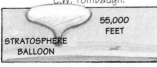

55,000 FEET

STRATOSPHERE BALLOON

1932 Auguste Piccard (Belgium) establishes an altitude record.

1936 Around the world each week 250 million people go to the movies.

1907 1980 Mauchly & Eckert 1919

In 1946 two University of Pennsylvania engineers, Presper Eckert, Jr., and John Mauchly, co-invented the first general-purpose electronic digital computer.

The ENIAC (Electronic Numerical Integrator and Calculator) enabled the U.S. army to speedily calculate its artillery firing charts, by reducing calculation time from one year to about two hours. The ENIAC weighed nearly 30 tons. Its 18,000 electronic valves needed so much electricity that lights in a local town dimmed when it was in use.

After ENIAC, Mauchly and Eckert introduced EDVAC (Electronic Discrete Variable Automatic Computer), which was capable of changing stored instructions and altering its own program. This machine was followed in 1950 by UNIVAC (Universal Automatic Computer), for use in business.

The Computer Age had begun.

1941 Konrad Zuse invents the first computer with electromagnetic relays and punched tape for entering data.

1943 Alan Turing and others develop an electronic calculating device to crack wartime German codes.

1940 Printed circuits used for electronic equipment.

1942 John V. Atanassoff and Clifford Berry's computer is a forerunner for all later designs.

OURS WAS REALLY THE FIRST MODERN COMPUTER BUT WE ENLISTED FOR SERVICE DURING WORLD WAR II. THE WAR STOPPED US BEING FIRST!

MAYBE I'LL PRESS THIS ONE . . .

1948 Georges de Mestral discovers the idea of Velcro-fastening after a walk with his dog.

1947 Willard Libby uses the carbon-14 method for dating archeological objects.

I DON'T FEEL A DAY OVER 10,000 . . .

1945 Willem Kolff develops the first kidney dialysis machine.

1947 Dennis Gabor (England) outlines the idea of holography though it will need lasers (1960s) to make it work.

1948 Peter Goldmark invents the long-playing record.

THE ENIAC COMPUTER COULD MAKE 5,000 ADDITIONS AND 300 MULTIPLICATIONS PER SECOND.

1947 The Dead Sea Scrolls—documents in Hebrew and Aramaic from Christ's time—are found by two shepherd boys.

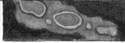
1942 Reber makes the first "radio" maps of the universe.

1947 The first supersonic airplane flight takes place in America.

1948 The term "bug" (meaning a computer malfunction), is coined in Manchester, England, when a moth supposedly gets into electronic circuitry.

1940 The Tacoma Narrows bridge collapses because it is not aerodynamically stable.

1941–1945 Millions of Jews and other victims of the Nazis are killed in concentration camps.

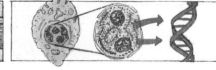
1944 Avery, MacLeod, and McCarthy say that DNA is the hereditary material for most life.

1940–1945 British cities "blitzed" (bombed) by the Luftwaffe during World War II. German cities are bombed in return.

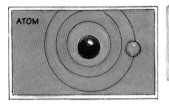
ATOM

1901 Enrico Fermi 1954

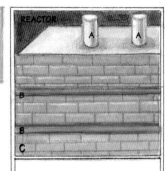
REACTOR

In 1938 Italian physicist Enrico Fermi went as a political refugee to the United States, where he worked as an atomic researcher. In 1942, with his fellow researcher Leo Szilard, he succeeded in building an "atomic pile" in a squash court at the University of Chicago. The atomic pile was the first atomic reactor. It used uranium to create the first nuclear chain reaction.

This was Fermi's first attempt at fission—the splitting of an atom's nucleus into fragments, which releases energy. It produced only half a watt of energy, but it was an important step: It enabled scientists working on a secret project during World War II, code-named the Manhattan Project, to successfully develop an atomic bomb.

The work of Fermi and his group also enabled other physicists to develop modern reactors capable of generating huge amounts of nuclear energy.

A. Fuel rods—cylinders of uranium.

B. Cadmium rods to absorb neutrons and control fission.

C. Graphite, to act as a moderator.

1947 Edwin Land invents the Polaroid camera.

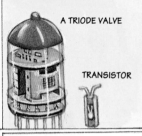
A TRIODE VALVE

TRANSISTOR

1947 Shockley, Brattain, and Bardeen invent the transistor. Tiny transistors replace valves, enabling scientists to make smaller computers.

1943 The first SCUBA (self-contained underwater breathing apparatus) is developed when Emil Gagnan adds a regulating valve to Jacques Cousteau's Aqua-Lung.

1947 R. Buckminster Fuller patents the geodesic dome.

FERMI WAS ONE OF THE MOST IMPORTANT MEN OF THE NUCLEAR AGE.

1943 Penicillin is first used in the treatment of chronic diseases.

1944 Germany launches the V1, a flying bomb, and the V2, the first long-range ballistic missile.

1945 The United Nations is founded and based in New York.

1941 Japanese planes attack a U.S. naval base at Pearl Harbor, Hawaii.

1942–1944 "The Diary of Anne Frank" is written.

1940 Prehistoric wall paintings are found in France.

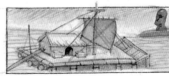
1947 Thor Heyerdahl sails a balsa-log raft from Peru to Polynesia.

1945 The U.S. explodes atomic bombs over Nagasaki and Hiroshima, ending World War II.

1910 CHRISTOPHER COCKERELL

Christopher Cockerell was a radio engineer turned boat-builder. His investigations into the problems of water-drag led to his inventing the hovercraft, or air-cushion vehicle, in 1955. Based on a wonderfully simple idea, it could fly over the surface of land and water on just a few inches of cushioned air. Cockerell developed his first simple model from an assortment of cans of different sizes, some kitchen scales, and a vacuum cleaner motor. When compressed air was pumped into a ring between the cans, it caused his model to lift and hover.

His SR–NI hovercraft, which at 65 knots could travel twice the speed of a traditional ferry boat, crossed the English Channel in 1959, exactly 50 years after Louis Blériot's first airplane flight over the Channel.

HIGH-FREQUENCY SOUND WAVES

1958 Scotsman Ian Donald uses ultrasound to study unborn babies.

1955 Chapin, Fuller, and Peterson develop a photovoltaic (solar) cell to make energy from sunlight.

1955 Narinder Kapary invents optical fibers in London, England.

1957 Sputnik I, the first artificial satellite, is launched by the USSR.

1950 Yoshiro Nakamata invents the floppy disk.

LOGICAL REASONING + FORMAL CALCULUS =

1956 Newell, Shaw, and Simon invent an artificial intelligence programming language.

SR·NI HOVERCRAFT NRDC

DOVER
CALAIS

THE HOVERCRAFT TEST FLIGHT TAKES PLACE 50 YEARS AFTER BLÉRIOT'S 1909 FLIGHT ACROSS THE CHANNEL.

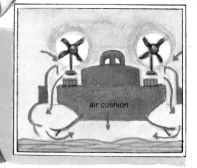
air cushion

THE DRAMATIC APPEARANCE OF THE HOVERCRAFT CAUSED A SENSATION.

1958 An American satellite successfully orbits the Earth.

1957 Gordon Gould first thinks up the possibility of lasers, but fails to patent his idea.

1958 NASA (National Aeronautics and Space Administration) is established.

1956 Jorn Utzon designs the Sydney Opera House, Australia.

1955–1956 Martin Luther King, Jr. campaigns for desegregation of the races in the U.S.

1953 James Watson and Francis Crick make a double-helix model for dioxyribonucleic acid (DNA).

I'M ALL SHOOK UP!
1956 The rock and roll era begins with singers like Elvis Presley.

GASP!!
1955 3D films are introduced.

1927 Theodore Maiman

The laser—Light Amplification by Stimulated Emission of Radiation—was invented by American physicist Theodore Maiman in 1960.

At first no one could think of many applications for the new invention, but by 1964 it was being used to perform eye surgery.

Today lasers are used in hundreds of ways: in industry, for cutting and welding; in engineering, for measuring and surveying; in medicine, for eye surgery and other operations; in military and space technology; in telecommunications, for carrying signals. Lasers are also used in computing, printing, and the production of compact disks and holograms.

1965 Doug Engelbart makes the first "mouse" to help operators interact naturally with their computers.

"UNIMATES"
1962 The first industrial robot is introduced.

HIGH FIDELITY
1967 Ray Dolby invents his system to reduce background sound on audio equipment.

ESSA-1
1960s NASA launches telecommunication (Telstar I, 1962) and weather (ESSA-1, 1966) satellites.

A NITINOL ELEPHANT NEVER FORGETS.
1960 Bueler invents Nitinol—a nickel-titanium alloy—which changes shape with temperature, but "remembers" its original molded shape.

NASA
1968 NASA recognition for Francis and Gertrude Rogallo's "Flexible Kite" design (used in space capsule landings).

light shield

mirror

semi-silvered mirror

glass jacket to cool laser

power

ruby crystal rod

released heat and red laser light energy

In the crystal rod, light energy excites the atoms, and they release energy.

"incoherent" light

flashlight

"coherent" light

laser

1964 The first lasers were used in delicate surgery, like the repairing of a detached retina in the eye.

AT FIRST NO ONE COULD FIND A PRACTICAL USE FOR MAIMAN'S LASER.

1968 Lake Erie pronounced "dead" from pollution.

1962 Rachel Carson's "Silent Spring" attacks pesticide pollution.

1969 Solar furnace at Odeillo in France.

ENVIRONMENTAL WORRIES BEGIN TO SURFACE • ECOLOGICAL AWARENESS • SUPPORT FOR RENEWABLE ENERGY

I KNOW PEOPLE THAT DENSE
1963 Theory of "Black Holes"— stars so dense that no light can escape the gravity.

VOSTOK I
1961 Yuri Gagarin of the USSR is the first man in space.

1969 Neil Armstrong is the first man to walk on the moon.

1963 President John F. Kennedy is shot in Dallas, Texas.

1960s Cold war tension between the U.S. and the USSR.

The SEVENTIES

1971 The microchip makes microcomputers possible.

1970 Floppy disk continues to be developed to store computer data.

No single inventor dominated the 1970s, but many exciting developments and much innovation took place.

In 1971 at Intel Corporation in Silicon Valley, California, Marcian Hoff invented the microchip. In 1972, the first pocket calculator, invented by Kilby, Merryman, and Van Tassel of Texas Instruments, became available. The first personal computer, the Apple II, appeared in 1979. And in 1979 Akio Morita of Sony invented the personal stereo, or Walkman.

Optical fibers enabled one single fiber to carry 20,000 telephone calls. Spy, information, and communications satellites beamed information back to Earth. Space probes gathered vast amounts of information about the planets. The Skylab and Salyut space laboratories were launched, and sent back information about our own planet.

1979 The Walkman, a portable miniature cassette unit with headphones, is devised by Akio Morita.

1979 Philips and Sony jointly develop the compact disk.

1971 The first magnetic levitation (maglev) train is developed in Japan.

1970s Using microprocessor (microchip) technology, MIT and Apple bring out personal computers.

1973 Liquid crystals are used for watch and pocket calculator displays.

1970s The USSR and U.S. set up space stations, space probes, and specialized satellites.

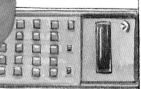

They send back detailed data from space by digital transmission.

1977 Fiber optic cables are first used for telephone systems.

1972 The pocket calculator.

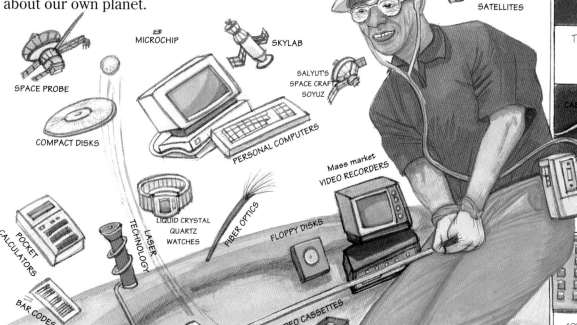

SATELLITES

MICROCHIP · SKYLAB

SALYUT'S SPACE CRAFT SOYUZ

SPACE PROBE

COMPACT DISKS

PERSONAL COMPUTERS

Mass market VIDEO RECORDERS

CABLE · QUARTZ GLASS

POCKET CALCULATORS

LASER TECHNOLOGY

LIQUID CRYSTAL QUARTZ WATCHES

FIBER OPTICS

FLOPPY DISKS

BAR CODES

VIDEO CASSETTES

AKIO MORITA WANTED TO LISTEN TO MUSIC AND PLAY GOLF AT THE SAME TIME.

110 stories

1974 Chicago's Sears Tower, the world's tallest building, is completed.

1974 Lucy, a 3-million-year-old hominid (early human), is discovered in Africa.

1976 In Seveso, Italy, a pesticide factory releases poisonous dioxins.

ENVIRONMENTAL ACCIDENTS IN THE 1970s

1978 The first "test-tube" baby is born.

1979 Partial meltdown at Three Mile Island reactor in Pennsylvania.

1970s Famine in Africa.

1979 The first case of a new virus, later known as AIDS, is recorded in New York.

1974 President Richard Nixon resigns over the Watergate scandal.

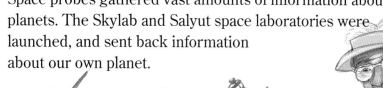

THE EIGHTIES

THE CRAY 1 CAN MAKE 150 MILLION CALCULATIONS PER SECOND.

Many earlier inventions were further developed in the 1980s. The supercomputer CRAY Y-MP, for instance, was now capable of carrying out 2 billion operations per second. IBM (International Business Machines) and Apple introduced the "mouse," a 1960s invention, to help users "talk" more easily to their machines. In 1984 Apple Macintosh introduced a powerful "user-friendly" desktop computer.

Industrial robots, another 1960s invention, were used in the 1980s for teaching, for factory work, and for evaluating dangerously irradiated areas of nuclear power plants. In Japan, Ichiro Kato built the WAHL-II, a two-legged robot.

In 1980s "virtual reality" was invented—with a "dataglove," a user could move three-dimensional objects on a screen and interact with the display unit or monitor.

SHUTTLE 1981

1980s NASA launches a reusable space shuttle.

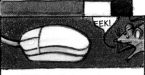

1983 Apple introduces a mouse and pull-down menu to its personal computers.

The first CRAY, 1976.
1980s Supercomputers ("number-crunchers") develop. By 1988 the CRAY Y-MP is able to make 2 billion calculations per second.

CANON

985 A laser color photocopier is invented using laser and computer technology.

Pressing the mouse from a certain location sends a particular command to the computer.

1983 The camcorder prototype is devised by Sanyo and Philips.

1980 Popular tiny aircraft—microlights—reach the market.

1980 Laser-read compact disk players are marketed as new sound systems.

1988 Thomas Zimmerman and L. Harvill develop a "dataglove" fitted with optic strands.

1988 The Joint European Torus machine reaches a temperature of 100 million K, 10 times hotter than the sun, in an attempt to show the feasibility of controlled nuclear fusion.

1980s IBM and Apple develop their personal computers (PCs). IBM (1981–1987) introduces DOS (disk operating system), a hard disk memory device, and a new memory chip to increase speed and memory. Apple's Lisa technology makes PCs powerful, but still affordable.

1980s Lasers are used for holography, medicine (arteries and tumors), and "smart" weapons.

1988 Müller and Bednorz invent a superconducting ceramic material that allows superconductors to work at warmer temperatures.

WHEN THE MOUSE IS MOVED AROUND ON A HARD SURFACE IT MOVES A CURSOR ON THE COMPUTER SCREEN.

1986 The Voyager aircraft flies around the world without refueling.

GLASNOST and PERESTROIKA

1980s Tropical rainforests are rapidly destroyed.

1980 Smallpox is eradicated.

FLIGHT

THE ENVIRONMENT

1980 New advances are made in genetic engineering.

1986 The space shuttle Challenger explodes just after takeoff, and its crew is killed.

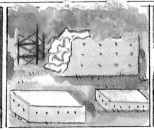

1987 Presidents Gorbachev and Reagan meet to discuss arms reductions.

1986 Chernobyl: a nuclear accident in Russia sends radioactive fallout over Europe.

1980 Solutions to environmental problems are actively sought.

Organic farming

Lead-free gasoline

Catalytic converter

1981 Cloning—replication of DNA (the carrier of genetic information)—is attempted.

THE NINETIES

Who will be the great inventors of the 1990s, and which of their inventions will surprise us most?

Scientists in the present decade dream of producing tiny optical computers with light particles to carry the data. There are hopes of "growing" biological computers, with data stored on individual molecules. We do not know if these developments will happen. But we do know that work on virtual reality, with the viewer partaking in a three-dimensional computer-generated world, is becoming more sophisticated, and that in Japan, trains may soon travel at speeds of over 340 miles per hour!

SUPER-CONDUCTIVITY

BIOLOGICAL COMPUTERS

IT'S FREEZING IN HERE!

COLD FUSION

VIDEO COMPACT DISKS

MAGLEV

VIRTUAL REALITY

LASERS AND TELE-COMMUNICATIONS

IN A VIRTUAL REALITY COMPUTER SIMULATION YOU NEED TO WEAR A SPECIAL HELMET AND DATAGLOVE.

1990 Germany reunites after the Berlin Wall is dismantled.   Revolutions and nationalism in Eastern Europe.   NASA plans to put a space station on Mars after the year 2000.

WHITES ONLY

CLIMATIC CHANGE

South Africa moves toward multiracial democracy after Nelson Mandela's release from prison.

CFCs AND OZONE DEPLETION   ENVIRONMENTAL PROBLEMS IN THE 1990s   POLLUTION

GLOSSARY

A

Aerodynamics   The study of the forces that act on bodies moving through the air.

Aerosol   Particles suspended in a gas (for example, a mist); or a substance dispensed from a pressurized container.

Ammeter/Amperemeter   An instrument that measures an electric current.

Anesthetic   A drug that causes the loss of sensation to pain, touch, and heat.

Animalcule   A microscopic organism.

Antiseptic   A substance that destroys or prevents the growth of bacteria and other microorganisms.

Archimedes' screw   A hollow tube with a screw-like device inside; when one end is placed in water and the screw is rotated, the water rises upward.

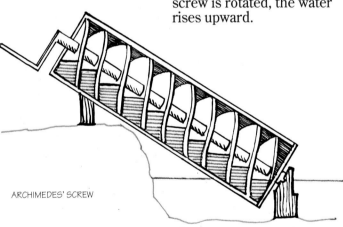

ARCHIMEDES' SCREW

Artificial intelligence   The idea that computers might be programmed to learn, reason, adapt, and self-correct, as humans do.

Asteroid   One of thousands of tiny, rocky, planetary bodies that travel around the sun between the orbits of Mars and Jupiter.

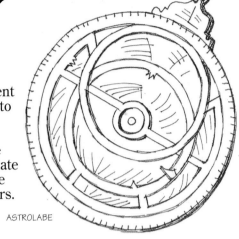

Astrolabe   An instrument used by early navigators to measure the altitude of the sun and stars; it can tell the time, find latitude and longitude, and calculate the future positions of the sun and the brightest stars.

ASTROLABE

Astronomy   The science of the universe outside of the Earth's atmosphere.

Atom   The smallest unit of a chemical element that has all the properties of that element.

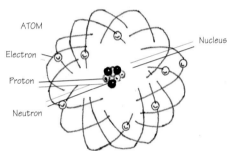

ATOM
Nucleus
Electron
Proton
Neutron

Atomic pile   Another name for a nuclear reactor (the pile is a stack of graphite blocks used to moderate a nuclear chain reaction).

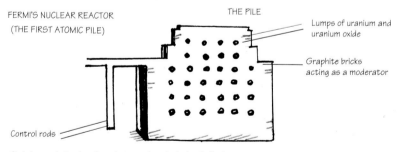

FERMI'S NUCLEAR REACTOR
(THE FIRST ATOMIC PILE)
THE PILE
Lumps of uranium and uranium oxide
Graphite bricks acting as a moderator
Control rods
Cadmium rods to absorb neutrons and control atomic fission

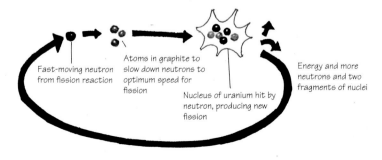

Fast-moving neutron from fission reaction
Atoms in graphite to slow down neutrons to optimum speed for fission
Nucleus of uranium hit by neutron, producing new fission
Energy and more neutrons and two fragments of nuclei

Axis powers   The alliance of Nazi Germany, Fascist Italy, and Japan from 1936 to its defeat by the Allies (led by the United States, Great Britain, the Soviet Union, and China) at the end of World War II.

B

Backstaff   An early navigational instrument used to measure the sun's altitude, so called because users have their back to the sun and look at a point of light shining onto a scale.

Bacteria   A large group of variously shaped microscopic organisms that can multiply rapidly and cause disease in plants and animals.

BACTERIA

Ballistics   The study of the motion of projectiles, such as bullets, shells, and missiles.

Barometer   An instrument that measures atmospheric pressure; it is useful for weather forecasting.

Bathysphere   A deep-sea observation sphere, usually made of steel, that is lowered into position by cable.

Battery   A device, usually made up of two or more connected units, that transforms chemical energy into electric energy.

Biological computer   A brain is a natural "biological computer," using living cells, or "wetware," instead of electronic "hardware," to process information. Artificial biological computers cannot yet be made.

Biology   The study of living organisms.

Bolsheviks   One of the two main branches of early Russian socialism, led by Vladimir Ilyich Lenin; the Bolsheviks seized power in 1917.

C

Calculus   A branch of mathematics that deals with the calculation of constantly varying quantities.

Calorimeter   An apparatus used for measuring heat.

Calotype process   An early method for making a photographic image, invented by William Henry Fox Talbot.

Camera obscura   A large box (literally a "dark chamber") with a convex lens at one end. The image of an object is focused on a screen at the other end, where it can be traced. The modern camera was developed from the *camera obscura*.

Camphor   A whitish substance originally distilled from the camphor tree and used, among other things, for making celluloid, a type of plastic.

Carbon-14 dating   A method of dating organic material such as wood, bone, ivory, or cloth, by measuring the amount of the radioactive isotope carbon-14 it contains.

Cartographer   A person who draws and prepares maps.

Cast iron   An alloy of iron, carbon, and other elements that is generally not malleable (able to be shaped with a hammer or a roller); it is usually cast (poured into molds) to make specific shapes.

Catalytic converter   A device that reduces the amount of pollutants emitted in a car's exhaust.

Cellulose   The carbohydrate substance making up plant cell walls; it is used in the manufacture of paper, fabrics, paints, and plastics.

Centrifugal force   The tendency of an object in circular motion to fly away from the center.

Cesarean section   Delivering a baby by cutting through the walls of the mother's abdomen and womb. Sometimes this method is safer for the baby.

Chain reaction   A chemical or nuclear reaction that produces energy or products that cause further reactions.

Chip   Popular name for an integrated circuit, made on a flat, wafer-thin section of silicon.

SILICON CHIP

Finger

Cinématographe An instrument for making "moving" pictures. Pictures of still photographs of moving objects are projected onto a screen in rapid succession, giving the illusion of motion.

Computer A programmable electronic machine that can store, retrieve, and process data.

COMPUTER INPUT EQUIPMENT

OUTPUT EQUIPMENT

Visual Display Unit

Keyboard

Keyboard and Mouse

Modem

Processor memory and related circuiting

Monitor

Printer

Modem

Floppy disk and disk drive

Floppy disk

File storage

Floppy disk   Disk drive

Cassette tape and tape drive

Cassette tape

Cassette tape   Tape drive

Condenser (in engineering) A chamber where exhaust steam from a steam engine or turbine is cooled and condensed to make a partial vacuum.

Conductor A material that allows the passage of an electric current.

Connecting rod In an engine or a pump, the rod connecting the piston and the crank.

Convex Having a surface that is curved or rounded outward, like a bulge.

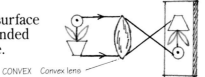

CONVEX   Convex lens

Copernican system The theory of planetary motion that says the sun is at the center of the solar system, and the planets (including Earth) revolve around it.

THE PTOLOMAIC SYSTEM DISPROVED

THE COPERNICAN SYSTEM PROVED TO BE MORE ACCURATE

Crank In a machine, an arm or lever that attaches one moving part to another; it is designed to convert one type of motion (such as up-and-down motion) to another (for example, the circular motion of a drive shaft).

Crankshaft The main shaft on an engine or other machine, on which one or more cranks are carried and are attached to connecting rods.

D

Dialysis The process of removing substances from a solution; dialysis is used to purify the blood of people whose kidneys have stopped functioning.

Digital computer A computer that uses coded on-off electrical signals representing digits (numbers) to solve numerical problems.

Diode An electronic device that allows current to flow in one direction only.

DNA Deoxyribonucleic acid; a double-stranded form of genetic material found in chromosomes. It stores genetic information and is responsible for transmitting hereditary characteristics from parent to offspring.

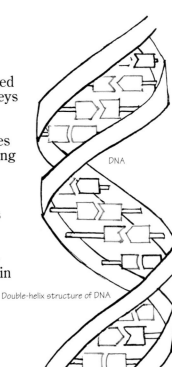

DNA

Double-helix structure of DNA

Dirigible   A navigable balloon or airship.

Dynamics   A branch of physics dealing with objects in motion and how they are affected by a force or forces.

Dynamite   A powerful nitroglycerine explosive packed into an absorbent substance to make it safer to handle.

Dynamo   A machine that converts mechanical energy into electrical energy.

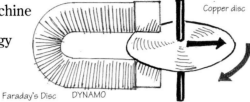

Faraday's Disc   DYNAMO
Copper disc
Electromagnet   Continuous electric current

E

Elasticity   The ability of a body to return to its normal size or shape after being stretched, contracted, or distorted.

Electrical motor   A device that converts electrical energy into mechanical movement.

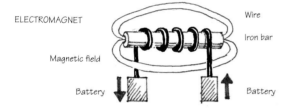

ELECTROMAGNET
Wire
Iron bar
Magnetic field
Battery   Battery

Electricity   Energy found in its most basic form in protons (positively charged) and electrons (negatively charged); an electrical attraction exists between two bodies that have opposite charges.

Electromagnet   A powerful magnet made up of a soft iron core wrapped with a coil of wire; the core is magnetized when an electrical current passes through the coil of wire.

ELECTRICAL MOTOR
Magnet
Magnetic field
Moving wire

Electron   Within an atom, the particle that carries a negative electrical charge.

Electronic devices   Devices, such as television tubes, electron microscopes, and silicon chips, that rely on the movement of electrons.

Embryology   The study of an animal or plant as an embryo—the stage of development between fertilization and birth, hatching, or germination.

Engine   A machine in which energy (the heat or chemical energy of fuel) is converted into mechanical work.

Engineer   *Civil*   A person who makes and maintains public works such as bridges, roads, and canals.
Mechanical   A person who makes and maintains machines.
Electrical   A person skilled in the production and transmission of electrical energy and the manufacture of electrical appliances.

CIVIL ENGINEER
Brunel

MECHANICAL ENGINEER
Benz

Visionary ideas, plans, calculations,
Good hands for dexterity

ELECTRICAL ENGINEER
Edison

Visionary ideas
Large head for brains, problem-solving etc.

Brains   Capacious pockets for earnings from many inventions

Euclid   A Greek mathematician who lived in Alexandria (in the 3rd century B.C.); author of a treatise on geometry.

F

Fermentation (in chemistry)   The slow decomposition of organic substances caused, for example, by microorganisms or enzymes of plant or animal origin; during the process, heat and gas are usually given off.

Fertilization   The fusion of a male reproductive cell with a female one, leading to development of an embryo.

Floppy disk   A lightweight, flexible magnetic disk that behaves as if rigid when rotated rapidly; used to hold information in a personal computer.

G

Galvanometer   A device for detecting and measuring the strength of a small electric current.

Gear   A moving part, such as a toothed wheel or lever, that transmits motion from one part of a machine to another.

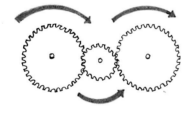

GEARS

Geiger counter   An instrument that detects and measures ionizing radiation, such as that emitted by radioactive materials.

Graphite   A soft, black form of natural crystalline carbon, used in pencils, as well as in electrical, chemical, and nuclear processes.

H

Heredity   The transmission of qualities from parent to offspring, through the DNA in the genes.

Holography   A photographic technique using lasers that gives a three-dimensional picture of an object.

Hydraulics   The branch of science that deals with the flow of fluids; for example, the use of pressurized water or oil to operate machines such as cranes and brakes.

Hydrofoil   A fast, light boat fitted with foils (finlike structures) on struts under the hull. At high speeds the foils lift the hull out of the water.

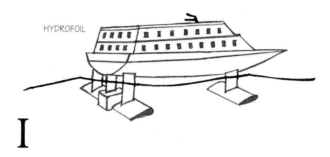

HYDROFOIL

I

Iconoscope   One of the first electronic TV camera tubes.

Ignition   The firing of an explosive mixture of gases, vapors, or other substances, usually by means of an electric spark (especially in the cylinder of an internal-combustion engine).

Internal-combustion engine   An engine in which the burning of a fuel (the mixture of air with gasoline or oil) takes place inside the cylinders and produces mechanical power.

INTERNAL-COMBUSTION ENGINE

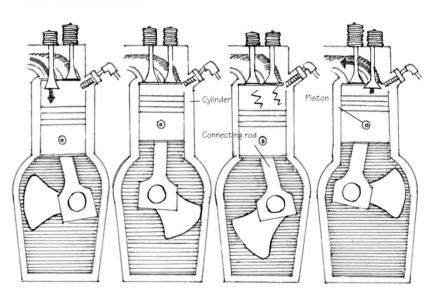

L

Laser (Light Amplification by Stimulated Emission of Radiation). A device that produces a narrow, intense beam of light of a single color, in which all the light waves are in phase.

Lathe A machine used for working materials such as wood, metal, and ivory by rotating them against a tool.

Lever A simple machine consisting of a bar that pivots on a fixed point (fulcrum).

LEVER

Lithography The process of printing an image from a stone or metal surface, using water and greasy ink.

M

Malleable iron Iron that can be shaped by hammering, beating, or rolling.

Manometer An instrument used to measure the pressure of a gas or liquid.

Mass (in physics) The quantity of matter in a body.

Microbe A microorganism, especially one of the bacteria causing disease or fermentation.

Microchip/microprocessor A computer's central processing unit (CPU), found in one or more integrated-circuit chips. It may be the main element of a microcomputer or a portion of a larger system.

Microcomputer A small, usually inexpensive computer that uses a microprocessor.

Molecule The smallest particle of a compound that has all the chemical properties of that compound; molecules are made up of two or more atoms.

N

Nucleus (in physics) The core of an atom, which contains most of the atom's mass. The nucleus is composed of protons (positively charged) and neutrons (no charge), and is surrounded by orbiting electrons (negatively charged).

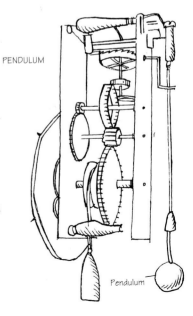

NUCLEUS

O

Offset printing The process by which the ink from a printing plate is received onto a rubber-coated cylinder, from which it is then transferred (offset) onto paper or another material.

Optical fiber A thin strand of pure glass that can transmit light by total internal reflection.

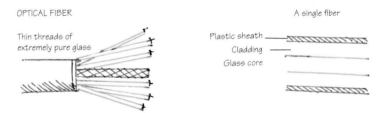

OPTICAL FIBER

A single fiber

Thin threads of extremely pure glass

Plastic sheath
Cladding
Glass core

Oxides A compound of oxygen with another element; often formed at a high temperature.

P

PENDULUM

Parabola A form of curve.

Pendulum A small, heavy body suspended from a fixed point and able to swing freely; a pendulum can be used to regulate the movement of a clock's works.

Physicist A person who studies the properties and nature of matter, the forms of energy, and the mutual interaction of energy and matter.

Pendulum

Piston   A short metal cylinder within a cylindrical vessel; it moves back and forth by fluid pressure (for example, in an engine) or it compresses and displaces a fluid (as in a pump).

Pneumatics   The science of the mechanical properties of air and other gases.

Polarized light   Light in which the vibration of the electric or magnetic field is confined to one plane, as opposed to ordinary light, which consists of a mixture of waves vibrating in all directions.

Probability   The likelihood of an event occurring, measured mathematically.

Proton   Within an atom, the particle that forms part (or, in the case of hydrogen, the whole) of the nucleus. It has a positive charge, equal and opposite to the negative charge of the electron.

Pulley   A simple machine consisting of a wheel over which a rope, belt, or cable runs; used for transmitting force, as in lifting a heavy object.

R

Radioactivity   The property of atoms of some elements (for example, uranium, radium, and thorium) to emit radiation in the form of alpha particles, beta particles, and gamma rays.

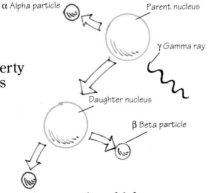

RADIOACTIVITY

α Alpha particle
Parent nucleus
γ Gamma ray
Daughter nucleus
β Beta particle

Radio waves   Electromagnetic waves by which messages are transmitted and received.

Receiver   The part of a radio, television, telegraph, or telephone that converts electrical or other signals into a message.

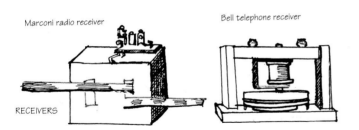

Marconi radio receiver
Bell telephone receiver
RECEIVERS

S

Steam engine   An external-combustion engine in which steam is the medium for converting heat into mechanical energy.

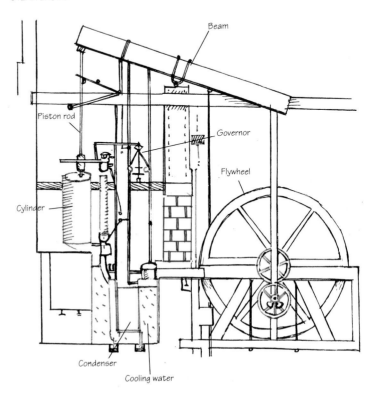

STEAM ENGINE

Beam
Piston rod
Governor
Flywheel
Cylinder
Condenser
Cooling water

Sterilization (of an object)   The process of removing unwanted microorganisms, using heat, radiation, antiseptic chemicals, or filtration.

Stratosphere   The atmosphere above the troposphere, where temperature does not decrease with altitude.

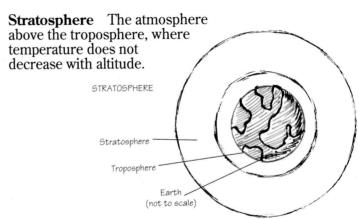

STRATOSPHERE

Stratosphere
Troposphere
Earth
(not to scale)

Supercomputer   A powerful, high-performance mainframe computer used for scientific computations.

Superconductivity   The property of some substances (some pure metals or metallic alloys) of having no resistance to the flow of an electrical current at very low temperatures.

Supersonic   Faster than the speed of sound.

T

Telegraphy   The old name for communicating certain material (words or pictures) at a distance. Wireless telegraphy is the transmission of signals through space by means of electromagnetic waves in the radio frequency range.

Television   The electronic transmission and reception of moving pictures.

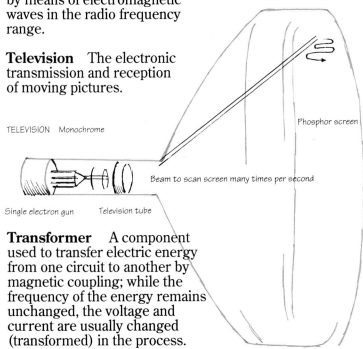

TELEVISION   Monochrome

Phosphor screen

Beam to scan screen many times per second

Single electron gun   Television tube

Transformer   A component used to transfer electric energy from one circuit to another by magnetic coupling; while the frequency of the energy remains unchanged, the voltage and current are usually changed (transformed) in the process.

Transmitter   The part of a radio, television, telegraph, or telephone that produces electrical signals to transmit a message.

TRANSMITTERS

Marconi radio transmitter

Bell telephone transmitter

Triode   A vacuum tube or electronic valve containing three main electrodes—a cathode, an anode, and a control electrode, or grid.

Troposphere   The lower part of Earth's atmosphere, from the planet's surface up to the stratosphere; in the troposphere temperature decreases regularly with altitude.

Turbine   An engine that uses a continuous stream of fluid (gas or liquid) to turn a shaft and create rotary motion; turbines produce power for such machines as ships, aircraft, and electrical generators.

U

Ultrasound   Sound with a frequency above 20 kilohertz (20,000 cycles per second); used by bats and dolphins to locate objects, and by humans for medical purposes such as scanning tissues.

V

Vacuum   A space entirely empty of matter. On Earth, only a partial vacuum is possible.

Virtual reality   Computer-based systems that allow users to explore imaginary environments.

Vulcanized rubber   Rubber treated with compounds such as sulfur that make it more elastic, stable, and durable.

W

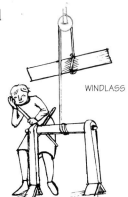

WINDLASS

Windlass   A device for hauling and hoisting; basically a cylinder wound with rope and turned with a crank.

X

X-rays   Short-wavelength electromagnetic waves, produced when high-speed electrons strike a solid target; x-rays can penetrate solids and ionize gases.

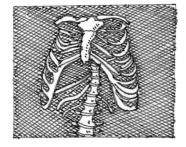

·INDEX·